im
dd this thread
to your own already
woven discourse.
Thanks!
Ivan Kane
7/27/01

Neither Beasts
nor Gods

Neither Beasts nor Gods
CIVIC LIFE AND THE PUBLIC GOOD

by
FRANCIS
KANE

SOUTHERN METHODIST UNIVERSITY PRESS
Dallas

Requests for permission to reproduce material from this work should be sent to:
    Rights and Permissions
    Southern Methodist University Press
    PO Box 750415
    Dallas, TX 75275-0415

Library of Congress Cataloging-in Publication Data

Kane, Francis, 1944-
    Neither beasts nor gods : civic life and the public good /
by Francis Kane.
    p. cm.
    Includes bibliographical references and index.
    ISBN 0-87074-422-4 (cloth). — ISBN 0-87074-423-2 (paper)
    1. Common good.   2. Public interest.   3. Political participation.
I. Title.
    JC330.15.K36   1998
    320'.01'1—DC21   97-33188

Cover art by Barbara Whitehead
Design by Tom Dawson Graphic Design
Printed in the United States of America on acid-free paper

10   9   8   7   6   5   4   3   2   1

This book is dedicated to the memory
of Martin, our son (1973–1989):

...δ' ἄχος αἰὲν ἄλαϲτον κείνου

Homer, *Odyssey*

ACKNOWLEDGMENTS

I would like, first of all, to acknowledge all my colleagues and students at Salisbury State University whose conversations helped initiate, nurture, and bring to completion this work. Especially, I want to thank my dear friends Jerry Miller, Tony Whall, and Bill Zak, who read various versions of the work and whose criticisms and suggestions improved, immeasurably, the arguments within.

To William F. May, without whose encouragement and support this work would never have come to be, I owe an incommensurable debt. His own craft as a writer, so limpid and literary, inspired my own very modest emulation.

To the editorial staff at Southern Methodist University, in particular to Suzanne Comer, who initiated the idea for the book and, although she died all too untimely, is still fondly remembered, and to Kathryn Lang and Freddie Jane Goff, who so expertly and graciously brought it to completion: to all these fine people I am most grateful. Heartfelt gratitude must also be extended to my sister, Mary Sullivan, and to my secretary, Libby Collins, both of whom labored tirelessly over the manuscript. Thanks also to a dear old friend, Mike Ruggeri, who, knowing my difficulties in getting started, offered perhaps the wisest advice: "Write the introduction last!"

Finally, I want to acknowledge the wonderful support and love of my family, both immediate and extended, particularly to my parents, my wife, Mary, and my sons Gabriel, Timothy, Daniel, and Terence. Aristotle remarked that the first community is the household where the members share their bread together. I think, too, all good conversation, at least in our Irish-American household, begins at and winds its way back to the dinner table.

CONTENTS

Weavers and Sailors

‿

L et me begin by invoking two heroic arts of the ancient Greeks: weaving and sailing. Any thinker who tries to speak significantly about politics today could certainly use the patient cleverness of that master weaver Penelope and the daring resourcefulness of the great navigator Odysseus. Plato's fondness for employing navigational metaphors in his political philosophy is well known; but a line in his last great work, *The Laws*, evokes the common thread that runs through and unifies this book. What "knits together" a community, the wise old thinker mused, is "not private interest but the common good (the *koinon agathon*)."[1]

It would be difficult to mention any political issue today—whether health care or abortion, welfare reform or assisted suicide—that does not presuppose the civic understanding of our common purpose. The idea of the common good, however, has until very recently been barely acknowledged, if not outright rejected, by political pundits. The more recent inheritors of the classical liberal tradition, who posit individual rights as their theoretical centerpiece, have often treated with suspicion and even hostility any attempt to define a good that might be common to each and every citizen.

Individualism, though, ties a community in knots, and American individualism is foundering on its own premises and exhausting itself in the conflicting demands of purportedly autonomous individuals. What common bond (other than what an individual wants, an individual gets) can there be in a community where citizens assert at one and the same time the right to live and the right to be dead, where it is not deemed inconsistent to want to abolish capital punishment and institute assisted suicide? Conservatives and liberals alike, free market economists and pro-choice liberals, all of us are descendants of the eighteenth century (classical liberal) tradition of atomistic individuals for whom the public good is subordinate to private interest.

Fortunately, the winds of individualism seem to be abating and there is ample evidence of a fresh breeze billowing from another direction. Writers as diverse as Robert Bellah, Wendell Berry, Michael Novak, William Galston, Marcus Raskin, and Amitai Etzioni have all hearkened back to the idea of the public good.[2] These recent efforts call up memories of an earlier movement in the 1950s called "public philosophy." As defined by the two great spokesmen of that movement, Walter Lippmann and John Courtney Murray, the task of public philosophy was to bring to bear the principles and substantive truths of a democratic polity upon the specific issues of the day.[3] In the words of one public philosopher, Richard Bishirjian, "politics is something more than deciding who gets what, when and where . . . [it is] also the resolution of questions of a higher sort, such as what is good for the community as a whole."[4]

Though it did not always bear that name, the threads of a public philosophy can be traced back through our history to the founders' evocation of the "publik good" and, even further, back to the scholastic idea of the *bonum commune* and the Ciceronian *res publica* (the public thing), back, finally, to Aristotle and Plato, to the early Greek dramatists and to that heroic bard who stands at the very beginning of the western tradition, Homer.

In the following chapters, I will be drawing upon that immeasurably rich tradition. Good weavers, all, those thinkers provide me with the guidance to fulfill my purpose in this work: to shed some light on our shared public lives. To do that, I will, first of all (in chapter 1), attempt to untangle the knotted cord of individualism that binds each citizen to his or her own private agenda. The case of Elizabeth Bouvia, perhaps the earliest legal request for assisted suicide in America, will be an instructive paradigm. Even more intellectually daunting, but no less necessary, is the effort (in chapter 2) to reweave a sense of the public good that relies not on any a priori metaphysical assumptions but rather on a phenomenological description that pays strict attention to the meanings already embedded in our public transactions. The fabric of the public good, if it is to be efficacious, must be finely meshed with the character of the citizens (chapter 3) and embroidered with eloquent, persuasive speech (chapter 4) and finally displayed in democratic action that invites all citizens to participate (chapter 5).

Invoking the extensive tradition of public philosophy does not, unfortunately, tell us *how* to do it today. If one must be a bit of a weaver in knitting together an account of the public good, a bit of sailing expertise would help in tacking back and forth between the shoals and eddies of so-called postmodern thought. In fact, entering into contemporary debates about philosophical method is like tacking of old between Scylla's rocks and Charybdis's whirlpool. Given those bleak prospects, I am tempted by a certain boyish impishness to take a few furtive glances to make sure no theoretician is looking and then just quickly launch my skiff. Actually, that is what I pretty much will do—knowing that citizens suffering the immense task of living together will find debates about theoretical methodology rather beside the point. The requisites of good philosophical argument necessitate, however, that I make some remarks on how I intend to sail these rather treacherous waters.

First of all, I try to steer clear of hardened ideological positions on the one hand and a plastic relativism on the other. An ideological approach reduces public philosophy to a mere instrumental exercise; given certain dogmatic premises (from either the political left or right), the ideologue deduces his or her position on whatever issue is at hand. So, if one opines that the United States is a demon of imperialism or, conversely, the manifest hand of God on earth, then whatever enterprise this country embarks upon will be, depending on the applicable dogma, blamed or praised.[5] I want, by contrast, to pay as much attention as possible to the actual reality of our public lives without ideological blinders. Conversely, a relativism that disdains any moral judgment would refuse to look at the possibility that acts such as genocide, rape, and child abuse are universally and definitively evil. While hardly innovative, my efforts here will try to show how self-defeating and enervating that position (if it can be called that) is.

Executing the initial methodological tack between two obvious extremes is considerably easier than subsequent maneuvers.

Because public philosophy is a hybrid of theory and practice, it will of necessity always look uneasily in two opposite directions. It will want to cast a theoretical glance backward to locate some reference points on which to rest its more practical conclusions. Likewise, it will always want to rush ahead to tackle specific policy issues. Tugged too far backward or too quickly forward, the skiff of public philosophy would too easily flounder. The search for foundational principles, for example, may not be futile but certainly can be a distraction from the specific vocation of the public philosopher: to articulate and analyze the current commitments of the civic community. To rush forward without attention to the principles of a good polity, however, would only lead us to shallow, muddied positions. I will steer a persistently middle course, content to sail in that tension between backward and forward forces. My reasons for doing so should become evident as the discussion proceeds; at this point, however, I will comment briefly on how my own view resembles and yet departs from two intellectual viewpoints that have also struggled with the methodological dilemma: the natural law theory and the narrative approach in ethics.[6]

In the 1950s, John Courtney Murray and Walter Lippmann operated out of an explicit natural law perspective, grounded in a view of unalterable human nature and ultimately residing in (for Murray at least) a religious belief in God, as Creator and Giver of life. That traditional approach was, for these thinkers, infinitely better than the alternatives: a self-defeating relativism, an emasculated positivism, and a doctrinaire Marxism. Murray, more the philosopher than Lippmann, took great pains to validate the natural law approach, but at the end of his great work, *We Hold These Truths*, he confesses that it took so long to establish natural law as the ground for public philosophy, he had "no time or space to develop it."[7] The intervening decades have hardly created a climate any more congenial to his natural law approach; the criticism that public philosophers rely too heavily on truths extrapolated from metaphysical assumptions continues to be a hard one to shake. More recently, William Sullivan has argued the case for public philosophy based on an extensive and effective critique of liberal individualism. However, even that work, *Reconstructing Public Philosophy*, is devoted almost exclusively to the historical and philosophical argument for reconstituting public philosophy and only hints at what doing it might entail.[8] While significantly indebted to these earlier efforts and, indeed, guided by them, I, nonetheless, would like to steer away from both extensive metaphysical speculation and historical criticism and concentrate rather on the nature of our human transactions as revealed to us by our common experience.

To skirt these foundational pitfalls, another group of more contemporary thinkers prefer to operate out of a particular tradition which is formed by story rather than a rational account.[9] In this so-called narrative approach the moral commitments of a community are teased out of the stories that define and characterize the particular tradition; for example, the gospel narratives for the Christian faith. While the particular tradition is accepted as authoritative and definitive by the believers of the story, there can be, so these thinkers argue, no universally definitive story. Indeed the very particularity of the narrative would preclude any claim to universality.[10] American public philosophy, rooted as it is in the American foundation and experiment, relies for its inspiration on those particularly American narratives. I, too, will draw heavily on specific stories to help shed light on the meaning of our shared existence. But just as the natural law philosophy has been tarred with the perception, at least, of dogmatic assumptions, the narrative approach has been unable to shake the nagging criticism of its own arbitrariness. Curiously enough, most of us who live within and accept a narrative tradition, whether religious or political, believe that such a tradition is worthy of our commitment because it speaks to the profound hopes and deepest longings of every human being. Moreover, if public philosophers are called to be critical of their own narrative, then there must be a way of gaining some distance from our particular situations. For the crucial purposes of living together, we have to be able to distinguish between a narrative like *Eyes on the Prize* and a *Mein Kampf.* Narratives are, after all, narratives of . . . something. My own efforts will be to explore the meaning of those human transactions which constitute narratives in the hope that some moral judgments can be tendered, however tentatively, about them.

The above comments are not meant to be rejections of the natural law and narrative approaches; indeed, I find both traditions a source of rich material about our public life. Rather, I mention them and hint at some of their perceived limitations to locate better my own course and to indicate why I try to steer away from executing a series of foundational turns on the one hand or arbitrarily adopting a particular narrative on the other. My own via media tries to pay as much attention as possible to the lineaments of our public transactions. In this delicate tacking maneuver, fortunately, there are a few able navigators. I have found the phenomenological movement in general, with its careful "letting be" of things, and Hannah Arendt's own particular phenomenology of human action most helpful guides. Since I find moral categories embedded in the very lineaments of all our public transactions, I look also to Aristotle, for whom ethics and politics constituted a single discipline. One more recent work, Robert Sokolowski's *Moral Action*, masterfully articulates, from the perspective of the early phenomenologist Edmund Husserl, the meanings embedded in our moral acts.[11] This book, which attempts "to trace the categorialities, the forms of thinking, that occur in human action and that constitute it as human action . . . and to display the identifications and differences whose presence is required if there is to be human action at all," convinced me of the possibility of doing public philosophy in the way I have tried in this book and particularly helped me to traverse the methodological obstacles mentioned above.[12]

At this point, a brief example might help give the reader a more concrete sense of my own approach. A few decades ago public education became embroiled in the controversy over teaching values in the classroom. The context of the public debate (at least in its broadest brush strokes) was the breakdown of the old school's somewhat doctrinaire and moralistic approach to learning. The new, more pluralistic "value-free" approach swept away the old order and left us with the paper-thin clothing of values-clarification exercises. It is pretty much accepted today that both approaches are seriously flawed. What alternative approach would undo the bankrupt values-free approach without slipping back into an arbitrary dogmatism was a difficult question for those concerned with the moral crisis in our society and civil liberties.[13] One obvious solution, asking parents, educators, citizens, and the students themselves what values they hold and then trying to achieve a consensus about a list of commonly held ones, has met with some success in various county school systems. Such an approach, though, would still be vulnerable to the criticism that it might create a "tyranny of the majority" in which the values of minorities might be excluded. If, as part of the whole process, we were to pay close attention to what goes on when learning takes place and tease out the values implicit *in* education itself, we would be less open to the charge of imposing a values agenda from the outside. For example, if an educator is going to teach history, how could that be done if not within the context of truthfulness and fairness? When an educator objects to the teaching of values in the public schools, I inquire only whether he or she forbids cheating on exams. Honesty, justice, tolerance, respect for others—all these and other values are implicit in the learning process itself and provide a way of negotiating the tricky question of "whose values?" in public education. I offer this example not because it represents some magic bullet that would resolve all our public arguments about education; in fact, such a "method" can at most provide the framework for the arguments that will ensue. What it does reveal, however, is how moral purposes are embedded in our activities and need not be always construed as some arbitrary or dogmatic imposition from outside. That approach, broadly termed phenomenological, will guide my investigations. Having said that, I will leave these methodological musings, recognizing that some hermeneutical questions will inevitably go begging. At this point, though, I would prefer to follow Nike's advice and "just do it." Failures in methodological precision can be offset, or so I hope, by any success I might have in addressing issues head on and persuading my fellow citizens of the worthwhileness of good public argument.

If the reader can indulge me two more brief tacking maneuvers, we can then set sail for open waters. These reflections will move rather freely (perhaps scandalously for some academics) between our current political lives and those of the ancient Greeks. I do this in an effort to create perspective and depth. Since they stand at the beginning of the Western tradition, the Greeks certainly are us but, in their wonderful strangeness, they are also not us. In that tension lies their creative power for us. I will make some mild demands on the reader because of my use of Greek terms. I do so not out of any effort to impress you with my erudition (I am no classicist), but I do believe that by paying attention to this ancient language we can rediscover the meaning of our sometimes lost political culture. To nurture a dialogue between the ancient and modern worlds, one that works *both* ways, can bring for those who travel back and forth in that conversation no small measure of wisdom.

A final note about my own political position. As I have already mentioned, I try to avoid the ideological arguments of both left and right while establishing some principles that emerge from a closely watched analysis of our public interactions. My stance, then, might be called "middle of the road." That is acceptable as long as the reader takes seriously what I have to say throughout about the subtly rich Greek notion of "the mean." At any rate, a stand I take on a particular issue is not nearly as germane to my purpose as is the development of the context out of which any fruitful public argument can emerge. As John Courtney Murray often pleaded, good argument only begins after some consensus is found. That consensus was admirably identified in a recent book by a *Washington Post* columnist, E. J. Dionne. In *Why Americans Hate Politics* he calls for a new, or better, a *renewed* sense of politics based not on ideological commitments but on a shared "sense of the public good."[14] That expresses the theme rather nicely for the modest efforts that follow.

CHAPTER 1

The Contemporary Scene:
A Modern Antigone

⌒

To grasp that a true political art cares, of necessity,
not for the private but the common good—that is
hard to bear.—Plato, *Laws*

The Case of Elizabeth Bouvia

On September 3, 1983, Elizabeth Bouvia, a twenty-six-year-old woman suffering from cerebral palsy, quadriplegia, and severe arthritis, voluntarily entered Riverside County (California) General Hospital, ostensibly for the treatment of suicidal depression. In reality, however, she wanted no treatment. She hoped instead to enlist the hospital staff's assistance in her plan to starve herself to death.

What had brought this young woman to Riverside Hospital had been a depressing series of recent events—loss of job, inability to bear a child, a broken marriage, progressive deterioration of her body—so that now she wished "to just be left alone and not bothered by friends or family or anyone else and to ultimately starve to death." She had grown weary of what she called "a useless body."

Upon admission she announced her intention to refuse all nourishment, and that decision initiated a protracted court battle with the hospital and her physicians. Ms. Bouvia's claim, argued by her ACLU lawyers, was that she had a right to refuse treatment and determine her own care even if it meant starving herself to death. But the hospital staff argued that they could not cooperate in her suicide and, since she refused to be discharged, life-sustaining nourishment had to be maintained. On December 16, Judge John Hews ruled in favor of the hospital, declaring: "The Court has determined the issue in whether or not a severely handicapped, mentally healthy person who is not terminally ill has the right to end her life with the assistance of society. The Court concludes she does not."

The judge's decision, eventually upheld by the state's Supreme Court, did not end the battle. In the weeks following the decision, awful confrontations erupted between an adamant, frustrated patient and a wearied and depressed hospital staff. Ms. Bouvia refused to eat and the hospital obtained a court order to have her force-fed with a nasogastric tube. In one week alone she managed to pull the tube out three times and each time it was forcibly reinserted, often with the patient fighting and screaming her resentment.

Convinced that she could not win her case, Ms. Bouvia then checked out of Riverside Hospital on April 7, 1984, and departed for Mexico, where she hoped to find medical officials more receptive to her request. When her efforts were rebuffed, she checked into a seaside motel where, with the aid of hired nurses, she intended to starve herself. The nurses, however, were fearful of prosecution and reluctant to stay. After a long night of anguished discussion with friends, she changed her mind, checked back into a Tijuana hospital on Easter morning, and ate her first solid food in seven months.

Though still convinced of the rightness of her cause, upon her return to California she struck an uneasy truce with medical officials, and at one facility in particular, the Los Angeles County/USC Medical Center, she worked out a standard of care acceptable to both parties. That irenic hiatus was disrupted, however, when she was forced to transfer from the acute care facility to the more standard High Desert Hospital. Here, just a little over three years after Judge Hews's initial decision, another acerbic court battle was initiated, this time over the hospital's insistence on the insertion of yet another nasogastric tube to supplement what they believed was Ms. Bouvia's inadequate nutrition. This time, however, she claimed she was not trying to commit suicide and, indeed, demonstrated a willingness to take some food by mouth.

Though Judge Deering of the California Superior Court agreed with the hospital's contention that Ms. Bouvia was still trying to commit suicide, the Appellate Court, in April of 1986, reversed his decision and ruled in favor of Ms. Bouvia's right to refuse this particular type of treatment, arguing that decisions about the quality of life were "hers alone." While accepting the court's decision, the hospital continued its "rehabilitative" efforts to the point of threatening withdrawal of Ms. Bouvia's morphine pump as a punitive measure for not increasing her caloric intake. In the face of this badgering of the patient, the judge allowed a transfer back to the Los Angeles/USC medical facility.[1]

For all its considerable pathos, the melancholy story of a woman's anguishing confrontation with the medical establishment seemed, at first glance, no different from the scores of other "right to die" claims that have been urgently advanced in the courts and thrust into our national consciousness. The media certainly played the story that way—"the right to die vs. the need to care" as one weekly put it.[2] But closer inspection reveals that the issues are far more subtle and ultimately more significant than the by-now-acceptable right of terminally ill patients to die without overly aggressive and useless treatment. (At no point in this protracted struggle did anyone, including Elizabeth Bouvia herself, claim that she was in imminent danger of death, except of course by her own hand.) Rather, like a Sophoclean tragedy, her story is not what it first appears to be, and underneath the tangled thicket of motives and cross-purposes lie some deep and awful questions about who we are and what we stand for as a community. It is for this reason that I have chosen to begin with a case which admittedly breaks no new legal ground but remains, I believe, an ethical and political lodestone toward which some of the basic issues of public policy have gravitated. In this chapter and the next, then, I will attempt to mine the rich core of ideas embedded in this case, most notably Ms. Bouvia's appeal to individual right and Judge Hews's invocation of the common good. The balancing of these two poles, at once repelling the state's unwarranted intrusion into the private lives of its citizens and, at the same time, attracting those same citizens to the sweet joys and harsh sacrifices of community life, is what the American experiment is, in large measure, all about. In that delicate balance between "the public good and private rights" (the phrase is

Madison's) lies the peculiar genius and yet the most striking vulnerability of that experiment.[3]

It is an experiment that has become, fortunately, part of the American ethos, developing in successive generations a habitual sensitivity to both private and public good. Any abrupt shift in the balance is, I think, unlikely to occur. But a gradual, unwitting swing in the direction of private license or public control is always possible, and so each generation needs to be both vigilant and reflective, continually assuring that harmony is maintained and, when necessary, even rethinking the basis on which the balance is struck. It may be that in our own day our concerns have tipped in the direction of private interest and away from the common good. Even more alarming, however, is the claim, more often bandied about in academic circles but not without effect in practical politics, that appeals to a common good shared by all citizens are hopelessly outdated and even dangerously authoritarian. That viewpoint, undermining as it does the very notion of a public-private balance, forces us to think more deeply about those core ideas that have served as the foundation of our public philosophy. Before I can tackle that task, however, I need to set the contemporary scene, to let the drama of Elizabeth Bouvia's court battles restate for our time the timeless struggle between individual freedom and the public good.

The Negative Pole: Private Rights

I would like to begin my consideration of the Bouvia case with the second series of court decisions, which permitted her to refuse the nasogastric tube. I do that, in part, because that decision is less controversial. The right of a patient to spell out the limits of medical intervention is widely accepted. "No codes" and procedures for termination of life support systems have become commonplace. The fact that the debate no longer focuses on turning off respirators but has moved to the withdrawal of nutrition and hydration from patients in a persistent vegetative state and now swirls around physician assisted suicide indicates in a striking fashion how a public consensus can emerge, solidify, and then move on in the course of a few decades. At any rate, there was no new ground broken in the California Appellate Court's decision recognizing Bouvia's right to determine the scope of her treatment.

That right, of course, is not found explicitly in the Constitution, and even the right to privacy, which the Appellate Court appealed to, is a fairly recent extrapolation in Constitutional law.[4] Yet even if we do not minimize the considerable debate about the definition, extent, and limits of privacy now occurring in the public forum (as for example, in the contentious extension of its scope to include abortion), still the protection of some rudimentary sense of privacy which would encompass Ms. Bouvia's would by most accounts fall under the scope of the ninth and fourteenth amendments to the Constitution and would be further solidified by the common law notion of the protection of one's bodily integrity.[5] Whatever the legal arguments, the image of hospital personnel forcibly inserting a nasogastric tube into the frail body of this highly vulnerable woman simply because of their disapproval of her caloric intake does raise the specter of a paternalistic practice of medicine that violates the most fundamental premises of a liberal democracy. The latter's tradition of limited government means nothing if not the power to restrict state intervention about what is done to an individual's body. Surely, "to insure these rights governments are instituted among men" (Declaration of Independence), and it would seem that there is no more obvious nor firmer bedrock upon which public philosophy could stand than the tradition of civil liberty here specified as the right to restrict unwarranted medical intervention. Whether or not we really are on solid ground or mere shifting sands depends, however, on what we uncover when we probe more deeply the basis for our convictions about individual rights.

For the founders of the American Republic, there was no doubt about the ground on which they stood. To inquire of them on what truths our individual rights rest would prompt the now memorable response: "We hold these truths to be self-evident, that all men are created equal, that they are endowed by their Creator with certain unalienable Rights, that among these are Life, Liberty and the pursuit of Happiness" (Declaration of Independence). These self-evident truths were, for them, embedded in the tradition of natural and divine law which rested on a sure understanding of human nature. Out of that terra firma emerged the moral imperatives that guided the precarious task of living together. It is no less clear that today such confidence has eroded to the point that not only is the self-evidence of those truths openly doubted, a pervasive skepticism about any directive principles has seeped in and permeated the body politic. In the words of the eminent public philosopher John Courtney Murray, "We refuse to say as a people: There are truths, and we hold them, and these are the truths."[6] And since we don't, we render specious any claim about our inviolable human rights. How can we, for example, agree with feminists' charges about the evil of gender stereotyping unless we also believe (as some of them clearly do not) in the bedrock truth that all persons are created equal? Actually, we can take heart in such patent dissimulation because it is evidence of a truth claim that will dominate my reflections: despite all our abstractions and intellectual posturing, the reality of human nature and its injunctions upon us remain irrepressibly tenacious. Still, the examples just cited reveal the awful threadbare cloak that today covers our rights talk. To return to the Bouvia case: if no underlying truth about the human condition supports her claim to bodily integrity, then her "right" is merely a conventional one, without moral warrant and subject to the whim of governmental largess. Put in economic terms, we continue to transact moral business even though the standard of exchange, self-evident truths, is now no longer valued. "Retail sanity and wholesale madness" is Leo Strauss's colorful characterization.[7]

It could be argued that the "wholesale madness" created by the loss of our common currency fails to undermine the practical sanity of recognizing Ms. Bouvia's right to determine the course of her own treatment. That is true . . . but only as far as it goes. The legal verdict settled, correctly I believe, who had the right to decide; it said little about what was the right decision. (What little it did say, we shall see, was horribly muddled.) The language of private right is unable to illumine our communal responsibilities in a case like this. Indeed it can even serve as a deflection.

Tuned in as we are to the language of individual rights, Elizabeth Bouvia immediately wins our sympathy, much like Antigone in Sophocles' tragedy. Against the force of Creon's political authority, the modern tendency is to side with Antigone's defense of the private and familial. The more disturbing questions (surely raised by Sophocles) about her own intransigence, her martyrdom too quickly chosen, are shunted aside. So, too, crushed as Ms. Bouvia is by the insensitive treatment of the hospital staff, all questions about the wisdom of her choice are too easily forestalled. In fact, even to suggest that, like Antigone, she too may "not know how to bend before troubles" would surely invite the charges of intrusive moral-izing and insufferable paternalism.[8] Later in the chapter and, indeed, throughout the book I will attempt to critique in a more systematic fashion liberal individualism's tendency to delegitimize moral language. For now, let me at least raise some moral *questions* that I think legitimately bear on the issue. For example, what if, out of a palpable despair over her fate, Elizabeth Bouvia actually is endangering her own health? Are we morally off the hook by sim-ply and solely affirming her right to refuse the nasogastric tube? Questions of legal intervention aside, what are the ethical responsi-bilities required of the staff in a case like this one? Surely if the assessment is made that she is receiving better treatment at the Los Angeles/USC Medical Center than at High Desert Hospital, that involves more than a recognition of her right to refuse the nasogas-tric tube. Would our moral obligations toward disabled persons like Ms. Bouvia be discharged by simply affirming their legal right to determine the course of treatment?[9] Might not the unbending managerial approach of the staff at High Desert and the permissive decision of the court both reveal an underlying unease or even repugnance for those disabled and deformed? Do our vacillating ministrations—from managing her back to "normalcy" to letting her completely alone—voice, in the fashion of a Greek chorus, "our greatest fear about our own limitations"? Those words are from Mary Jane Owen, herself a disabled person, who challenges us to shift the focus from Elizabeth Bouvia's plight to our own insecuri-ties: "She has come to personify *our* horror of vulnerability, frailty and all the 'imperfections' of disability."[10]

Whether or not one agrees with Ms. Owen's assessment, the issue she raises and the questions I pose cannot be addressed by clarifying the plaintiff's legal rights. Freedom of expression is an analogous case. Even if it were an absolute right (which, of course, it is not), an appeal to it would hardly allay the moral and political concerns the community might have about obscene, racist, or sexist remarks. Would we as a nation be unconcerned if our youths all spoke of women in the same derogatory tones as "2 Live Crew"? Similarly, the concerns we have about the treatment of the disabled are hardly resolved by affirming their right to refuse treatment. I will return to this issue in the following chapter; for now I wish only to point out how even on the practical level a case like this pushes us to ask: "What do we as a people stand for?" And that question shifts us to the other pole of our analysis: the public good.

The Positive Pole: Public Good

If the second legal battle validated, if only legally, Ms. Bouvia's individual right to refuse the nasogastric tube, the first court decisions wrestled with the limit of her liberty in requesting an assisted suicide. The earlier litigation did not involve the protection of an individual against the intrusions of society but whether an individual could require society to execute her suicidal wishes. In the second litigation, the court consented to Bouvia's right to make a decision about her health care. From a legal perspective it was not required to pass judgment on the probity of her decision. In the earlier case, however, the public cannot so easily wriggle off the hook. We cannot assist her in a suicidal act yet somehow distance ourselves from the moral implications of that act. However much we may wish otherwise, we cannot, any more than Creon, ignore the claim this modern Antigone made upon us.[11] Our response to her could tell us a great deal about ourselves as citizens. We have to wrestle with the fundamental political issue of whether the public must invariably serve the individual will or whether the protection of life as a public good transcends the individual's own deeply felt desire. If it is to start anywhere at all, the consideration of the public good must surely begin here—where life and liberty intersect.

Judge Hews's decision (upheld on appeal) affirmed the public good and "society's interest in preserving life" over the "right to self-determination."[12] But that hardly resolved the issue. Dr. Kevorkian has seen to that. Given the pervasive and unrelenting pursuit of individual self-fulfillment in today's culture, it was inevitable perhaps that a request like Bouvia's be made. And, while she failed in 1983, it is hardly shocking that others have succeeded a decade and a half later. A public philosophy must explore, then, on what moral bedrock the priority of life over an individual's will might rest. If a line is to be drawn in this case between personal desire and the common good, then we need to be quite clear about where, how, and why it ought to be drawn. To do that we must first look into and evaluate those arguments that would extend Bouvia's right to refuse treatment to include the right to an assisted suicide.

Philosophically her case can be succinctly stated in the classic language of liberal thought: if "over himself, over his own body and mind, the individual is sovereign" (J. S. Mill), the conclusion follows that such an individual should have (in Hume's terse phrase) "the free disposal of his own life."[13] To mandate state assistance, Bouvia need only add the following principle (Bentham's): "The happiness of the individuals, of whom a community is composed, that is their pleasures and their security, is the end and the sole end which the legislator ought to have in view."[14] Given Bentham's *raison d'etat* and Bouvia's "pleasure" to end her life, justified by Mill's warrant, Bouvia could argue her state-assisted suicide would be neither morally nor politically different from laws that mandate assistance for disabled people in securing their right to vote, to be educated, etc. Judge Hews's denial of her motion could be viewed as a lingering vestige of an authoritarian culture that still presumes to dictate, in the name of a common good, what is good for the individual.

As plausible as the argument may seem, it overlooks one inescapable and ultimately self-defeating point: Elizabeth Bouvia's wish for a state-assisted suicide would inexorably end up violating other citizens' wish not to participate in that act. I have made this argument more extensively elsewhere.[15] Here I simply want to explain the point and then proceed in another direction. If the judge had mandated that a publicly supported institution, Riverside Hospital, cooperate with Ms. Bouvia's wish, then that decision and the precedent it would have set would have inevitably led to a considerable assault on the freedom of many other persons—not only doctors, nurses, and hospital personnel, but also citizens whose tax dollars support those hospital facilities. Given the absence of any overriding state aim to have Elizabeth Bouvia dead (none, of course, was claimed), the violation of other citizens' liberty to satisfy what is essentially a private wish could not be justified. Autonomy is a two-edged sword that cuts both ways.

To curtail the argument here—its sufficiency in negating Bouvia's claim notwithstanding—would be to leave the impression that the sole check upon one's autonomy is the autonomy of another. Yet that is not the only argument Judge Hews made, and with good reason. The fact that Bouvia's claim to autonomy could not be made without violating the autonomy of nurses, doctors, and citizens is not, I think, a peculiar irony of her particular situation. It reveals, instead, a common fault of political arguments that rest solely on the supremacy of individual autonomy. If the sole end of the state were, again in Bentham's language, the "pleasures" and "security" of individuals, then the state would serve only an instrumental function, a mere means to the fulfillment of individual desire. Not only does this line of thought neglect the reality that behind the cold indifferent mask of the "state" lie, sometimes at least, real citizens with consciences of their own, but it also completely eviscerates whatever meaning and substantive claim the public good possesses. In affirming the medical profession's obligation to preserve Ms. Bouvia's life over her right to self-determination, Judge Hews offered this warrant: "Our society values life."[16] With that pronouncement he instantiated the traditional notion of an American public good. What we stand for as a people, or so the judge claimed, is the inviolability of human life.

That the founders professed just such a public good is indisputable. "No other phrase, except 'liberty,' " notes Gordon Wood, "was invoked more often by the Revolutionaries than the 'public good.' "[17] It would be nothing short of preposterous to suggest that these founders, who were willing to risk "their lives, their fortunes and their sacred honor" in order to found a "new order for the ages" (*novus ordo seclorum*), advocated such an attenuated notion of the public good as Bentham's.[18] In fact, Madison argues as much in the

Federalist Papers. After recalling the origins of the Republic in "the previous blood of thousands spilled and the hard-earned substance of millions lavished," he goes on to argue that "*the public good*, the real welfare of the great body of the people, is the *supreme object to be pursued*; and that no form of government whatever has any other value, than as it may be fitted for the attainment of this object."[19] Even the founders' notion of liberty, undeniably strong, did not convey what it so often does today: "the uninhibited cultivation of individuality" (Strauss's phrase).[20] As a *natural* right, liberty sprung from the very nature of our common humanity and, as such, transcended individual whim. One had no right, for example, to sell oneself into slavery. Even the great spokesman of the liberal tradition, John Locke, distinguished between the "State of Liberty" and the "State of License" such that, as a person is "bound to preserve himself," he has not the "liberty to destroy himself."[21]

But if this law of nature, which enables us to distinguish between liberty and license, which prohibits the citizens from self-destruction, has, as we have seen, lost its directive power, how much more does the notion of the common good fail to enjoin our public consciences. If, today, we still keep up the pretense of "unalienable rights," when it comes to the "common good" we hardly even bother. Until very recently it had all but vanished, if not from public awareness then certainly from the theoretical literature. Just as the transcendent claim of inalienable rights has been reduced to the more immediate demand for individual preference, so the attenuated notion of the public interest, which is simply a collection of individual preferences, has replaced the fecund sense of public good. That is hardly surprising: if we are reluctant to define, in any substantive fashion, what constitutes the individual's good, how much more difficult would it be to articulate a good for the whole community. If the eighteenth-century tradition of natural right has been severely questioned, the classical and medieval tradition of natural law, on which rested the notion of common good, has been unqualifiedly rejected.[22] Consequently, appeals to a public or common good are often greeted with the suspicion that, since they are extrapolations from a now defunct world view, they simply mask a hidden private agenda that threatens to impose a particular notion of the good on others. Hence, Judge Hews's verdict could be inter-preted as the imposition of a narrow right-to-life agenda on those who do not share the assumptions of that philosophy. That may be. Certainly, some in the right-to-life movement who appeal *solely* to their own or their church's particular interpretation of the Scriptures do little to dispel that interpretation. An appeal to the Constitutional tradition makes more sense from a legal and politi-cal point of view, but we have already uncovered the shaky ground upon which that rests. Undeniably, there is a good deal of practical wisdom in the verdict of the court insofar as it prohibited a state-assisted suicide, but such prudence, as we saw in the second court decision, may simply deflect us from the unstable foundation on which our public affirmations rest.

A good deal more could be said, indeed needs to be said, about this case. (I shall return to it at the end of the next chapter.) For now, though, I would like to pause and take stock of these first tentative forays and decipher in which new direction we ought to be moving.

In many ways Elizabeth Bouvia's story is a paradigmatic case of the age-old clash of private interest versus the public good, an ancient reenactment of the struggle between Antigone and Creon. If Creon's *raison d'etat* overwhelmed Antigone's *raison de famille* in ancient Thebes, today the balance seems to have tipped in the other direction. But a victory for either would be purely Pyrrhic, at least in the eyes of Sophocles and the American Founders since they believed that the health of a community lies in delicately balancing these two poles. Actually, I believe that the two court decisions strike a fairly good balance in the Bouvia case. The deeper problem, how-ever, is that the underlying conditions which make such a harmony possible are little understood.

So where does that leave us? We could learn to live with, even become comfortable with, our schizophrenic world of "wholesale madness and retail sanity." We could even intellectualize our repression of the madness by retreating into a pluralism that dis-covers in smaller, particularized communities the common assump-tions needed to justify whatever claims we want to make. That might work—at least a number of contemporary theorists place their hope there.[23] But, of course, assumptions can and do conflict, and I suspect that unresolvable claims and counterclaims—witness the abortion debate—will only become exacerbated in such a polity. At any rate, I think that option too easily surrenders the argument. No doubt an appeal to tradition no longer is sufficient to sustain us. But an appeal to our political experience, the source itself of the tradition's wisdom, may be a viable option. If we return "to the things themselves," in this case our political experience, and "let it speak for itself" (favorite phrases of phenomenologists), perhaps we might find embedded there, rather than extrapolated from some metaphysical heaven, the very concepts like human nature, common good, and natural right that we need to sustain our efforts at balancing the political order.

That, at least, is what I propose we explore in the next chapter. To do that, though, without a guide would be foolish and presumptuous. I propose, then, employing Aristotle to escort us through the initial, quite difficult, part of our journey. Admittedly, he's no Beatrice. But there is no more astute, more trustworthy observer of our public interactions than the ancient Stagirite. And, while he lacks the charm and grace of Dante's guide, he is, like her, both modest and moderate. In the febrile climate of politics those qualities should stand us in good stead.

CHAPTER 2
_____

The Public Good: The Greek Mean
or Goldilocks's Chair
◊

A beginning must be made, first of all, that follows the natural starting
point of the investigation. Of necessity, either the citizens share (*koinōnein*)
all things, or they share nothing, or they share some things and do not
share others. That they share nothing is clearly not possible since political
organization (*politeia*) is a community (*koinōnia*) which at the very least shares
a space and where a single space there a single city (*polōs*) and where a single
city there the citizens are sharers (*koinōnoi*).—Aristotle, *Politics*

. . . As Shared

With his accustomed care for the obvious but often neglected
origin of things, Aristotle points out that our being together
as citizens is first and foremost a sharing.[1] Civic community
is defined by those things we hold in common. That we share is for
Aristotle a necessity, rooted (as we shall see later) in the very nature
of our humanity. What we share and how it is shared mark the various kinds and distinctive character of human communities.

It is almost commonplace nowadays to note that Aristotle's
beginning stands in sharp contrast to social contract theorists from
John Locke to the present who claim that the origin of politics is to
be found in a precommunal state of nature where atomistic individuals hold nothing in common save a rather abstract equality and an
indeterminate liberty. In this contractual viewpoint, community is
not a natural phenomenon but a result of convention, embedded
not in necessity but in consent. Such a consent presupposes an
autonomous individual who may or may not choose the possible

perils and potential delights of a shared existence. The historical precedents for these communities formed by contracts among isolated individuals were tenuous at best, but that did not overly concern eighteenth-century social contract theorists. Their purpose was always crystal clear, to establish a moral leverage point against which the tyranny of kings could be checked. Hence, the doctrine of individual rights. A modern social contract theorist like John Rawls goes even further than negative restrictions against unlawful authority; with him, the "natural" state of autonomous individuals is transformed into a logical device whereby individuals must choose behind a veil of ignorance, which cloaks any possible bias, the system of justice and procedures that will best insure fair opportunities for each individual.[2] In such an imaginative artifice individuals create a sort of born-again intellectual experience, divesting themselves of all that is naturally given, to be born anew in a world of their own making. In both the early and more recent versions of the social contract, theoreticians were, admittedly, concerned more with the communal arrangements established than with the autonomous individuals who did the establishing. But in this model, in which government is but an artifice, an instrumental good chosen by discrete individuals for their own security, it is only natural that practical emphasis would eventually be put less and less on the appropriate form of government and more and more on the individual for whom that government existed. And so was born (in popular culture at least) the "improvisational self." By that phrase the authors of *Habits of the Heart* gave name to the contemporary obsession for creating what was for Locke but a dim historical moment and for Rawls a mere logical convention: the autonomous self.[3] Such a self, now not a historical or logical given but something practically to be achieved, is the unwavering focus of countless self-help books and popular therapies. They offer strategies for "giving birth to oneself" by "breaking free from family, community and inherited ideas."[4] This unencumbered self needs no one, depends on no one, but rather creates itself from scratch, improvising its values as it goes along. Relationships now taken up are not the result of chance or inheritance but of choice and consent. It is, one might suppose, the supreme achievement of the "I"—to give birth to itself.

This is not the place for a full-scale analysis of, much less assault upon, the social contract theory and its contemporary incarnations. I simply want to point out that, however fruitful as an intellectual trope or practical as a therapeutic strategy, this rebirth as an autonomous improvisational self (whether in its eighteenth- or twentieth-century version) obscures and distorts our very real communal origin: i.e., our conception as the fruit of shared intimacy between husband and wife, our first growth in the sheltering privacy of our mother's womb and our birth into the familiar surroundings of our homes. From the very private sharing of domesticity that marks the familial community there is a natural though (as we shall see) discrete progression to the sharing of what the Romans called the *res publica* . . . the "public thing." Only in the abstract phantoms of our brain do we exist as autonomous individuals; in the real world, we live with, move among, and owe our very being to others. "There are some truths we do not see," the authors of *Habits of the Heart* conclude, "when we adopt the language of radical individualism."[5]

Not seeing the truth is bad enough. Acting on an illusion, however, is a far worse fate. So at a time when we have repressed what is nearest and most natural to us—our communal beginning—we blindly try to create an artificial beginning bereft of its natural moorings and nurturance. Perhaps the frightening culmination of the inception of the autonomous self is an artificially managed conception, like the "test tube baby," in which a self can be engineered into existence without the natural act of intercourse or the nurturing environment of the mother's womb. Even if, however, artificial insemination replaces natural generation, even if the petri dish is exchanged—however terrifying and lonely that would be—for the womb, it would still not indicate an escape from our communal origin; rather, the replacement of the family community by a cartel of reproductive technicians would signal a tragic shift not unlike what occurs when a republic degenerates into a totalitarian state.[6] I need not trace out that awful unraveling. My point is simply to remind us of our inescapable origin and destiny: to be is to be with others (the Roman *esse inter homines*).

Indeed to reject our humble origins would be much like denying our final end. While much has been written about our culture's dissimulation in the face of death, precious little attention has been given to the avoidance of our naked, unchosen beginning. Both events are painful reminders of our vulnerability and dependence—but in strikingly different ways. The reality of death, as the old saying goes, wonderfully concentrates the mind. It has a way of individualizing any and all who would but think on it. When walking "that lonesome valley," the self is forced to confront itself, by itself. By contrast, in conception the self is first formed by a shared intimacy, and in birth that new self is introduced into the full human community. If thought is the beginning of philosophy, then birth is the beginning of politics.[7] Like death, our conception and birth is a given, something unchosen. In the face of it, we remain totally vulnerable and completely dependent upon those with whom we share our existence. It is, to borrow a phrase from Charles Kingsley, our "noble shame." Less noble, of course, is the shameful denial of our dependency that leads to an exaggerated sense of autonomy and ill-fated efforts "to be master of all things" (Sophocles). Neither Antigone nor Elizabeth Bouvia is all that frightened or intimidated by death. Shameful to them perhaps are their tragic, unchosen births: one of incest, the other of a hideous genetic disease. They seem to thrust us away, and much like the Greek chorus we do all we can to accommodate them. In Bouvia's case, if we cannot manage her back to normalcy, we distance ourselves from her by consigning her, with faint praise for her courage, to an early grave. So, in the end perhaps even death was meant to be shared. "Our share of night to bear – Our share of morning": that is, as Emily Dickinson suggests, the lot of mortals.[8]

If, then, to return to Aristotle, our shared existence (*koinōnoi*) is an inescapable, fundamental datum, what is it that political communities (*politai koinōnoi*) share? Let me begin with two prosaic examples: Imagine we are standing outside a polling place on election day and observing the bustle of citizens entering and exiting, or imagine we are inside an American Legion Hall observing an old-fashioned "bull roast" or clambake sponsored by the local Democratic Club (Republicans can imagine themselves at a champagne brunch!). Obviously, these citizens are sharing, as Aristotle remarked, a common space and (I would add) a common time. But, if we wanted to give a full account of what is going on, to observe only that we share a common space and time would surely not be adequate. We would not be able to distinguish those civic activities from an assemblage of bees coming and going around a hive or a herd of grazing cattle.[9] (Political pundits might find the similarities between voters and bees, bull roasts and grazing cows too delicious to ignore, but the humor of course would be based on the incongruity that underlies the behavioral similarity.) At any rate, "mere locality," as Edmund Burke remarked, "does not constitute a body politic."[10] We need to describe how the space we share as citizens becomes our *polis* and the time we share our history. To do that, we must recognize that the meanings of activities like voting and campaigning are accessible to us only if we uncover the choices and intentions that are embodied in those acts. In Aristotle's words: "We can observe that every city (*polis*) is a community (*koinōnia*) of some kind and every community is formed for the purpose of some good" (*Politics* 1.1252a1). Purposes, then, are what distinguish a voting booth from a hive and a bull roast from a green pasture. Only a fool (and perhaps certain behavioral scientists) would attempt to give an account of voting and campaigning without asking the participants what they are doing and why they do it. Even if our actions embody a discrepancy between what we do and what we say we are doing (often pointed out by social scientists), that inaccuracy or, perhaps, hypocrisy (whether intentional or not) can be unmasked or accounted for only if acts embody or fail to embody intentions and choices. I may be at the bull roast, for example, not because I believe in the candidates and their platforms but because I want my construction contracts to continue after the election. The fuller meaning of my activity, then, would include an account of the purported honorable intention along with the hidden ulterior motive of political graft.

Such analysis makes it all the more clear why Aristotle argued that the distinguishing feature of our humanity is our ability to "give an account" (*logos*) of ourselves. "Of all the animals humans alone possess the power of *logos*" (*Politics* 1.1253a10). By *logos*, Aristotle does not mean the mere use of vocal chords to indicate pleasure and pain but the specifically human ability "to account for what is beneficial and harmful, just and unjust" (*Politics* 1.1253a14–16). It is then the *sharing* of the moral "perception of good and evil" that "constitute the household (*oikian*) and the city (*polin*) (*Politics* 1.1253a16–19). Without an account that noted the choices and intentions embedded in human interaction, we would be unable to distinguish not only the activity of bees and humans but also the different meanings of human acts, such as the coming and going of citizens from a polling place and the coming and going of customers from a bank.

Now I suppose much of this seems rather obvious to the ordinary citizen (although citizenship is hardly an "ordinary" state); but, as we have already remarked, the obvious, precisely because it is obvious, is often overlooked, and the beginning, as Aristotle remarks, while most important, is most difficult because "it is very small in size and therefore very hard to see."[11] Theoreticians, the supposed "experts in seeing," sometimes are so blinded by their preconceptions that they sheer off the richness of human interaction in order to make the phenomena fit their presuppositions. So, for example, some behavioral ethologists look only at certain primitive behaviors like territorality and pronounce humans no different than any other primate, all the while failing to see what Aristotle so clearly saw—that human living-together, unlike cattle grazing, means sharing our words and thoughts (*koinōnein logon kai dianoias*).[12] Why is it, Walker Percy once queried (with his customary lighthearted sagacity), that human beings alone among all the animals continually try to deny they are unique? In their efforts to reduce all action and speech to some primitive, instinctual, and determined response, these ethologists then fail to see the simple truth embodied in Murray's assertion: "Wolves do not argue the merits of running in packs."[13]

So far I have attempted to show that any account of the meaning of our civic acts must start from the inescapable datum of our communality as humans. And that communality must be more than just a shared geography and chronology; it must also involve shared intentions and purposes. Insofar as these dispositions of the subject are embedded in the lodestone of our acts, intentions and purposes are not, then, extrapolations from some sort of metaphysical heaven but constitute the very meaning of what we do. Following this thread of thought we need to inquire next, what specific purposes do civic communities give to account for their existence? We might see this question as an extension of the old Socratic dictum "Know thyself." We need to know who we are as a community, and that implies rendering an account of our acts and their purposes.

Earlier I hinted at the distinction between voting and a bank transaction. Let us look at that distinction a bit more closely now because it will reveal an important difference between kinds of purposes. If I withdraw money from a bank for the purpose, say, of taking my family on vacation, the meaning of the bank transaction is thereby disclosed as instrumental; that is, I am doing this *in order to* achieve that. The full meaning of my act lies in an intention which outstrips the bank transaction. The bank transaction is not part of the vacation but is related to it as a means to an end. I am withdrawing money only because I intend to take my family on this vacation. On the other hand, if someone asked me why I was voting I could answer, "Because I am a citizen." Here the act of voting is done for the sake of civic participation. As such, it is the very embodiment of citizenship, for whatever else citizenship means (and it should mean much more) it at least implies that I am enfranchised to vote. Of course I vote in the hope that my candidates will win and even that certain good consequences will occur in the body politic. But those intended outcomes are not separate as the bank withdrawal and the vacation were; rather, the act of voting includes within it those very hoped-for consequences. If voting is more than just a mechanical act, it represents the fruit of my scrutiny of the candidates and the debate of the issues; it embodies my support of what the candidate stands for and my assessment of how well he or she will represent me. Furthermore, even if my candidate isn't likely to win or there's no hope he or she will win, that would not render my voting meaningless in the way the bank withdrawal would be if I didn't go on vacation. (How else does one explain the indomitable Harold Stassen or my vote for McGovern in the 1972 election!)

Now voting *could* be viewed instrumentally. I might sell my vote, for example, in order to buy a few drinks at the local bar. While it may not be of any great significance in certain activities to change the intention from doing something for its own sake to doing it in order to achieve a goal—for example, I might work out in the gym in order to impress my significant other rather than doing it just for fun or for the sake of my health—certain instrumental intentions could be so alien to the intrinsic or embodied meaning of the act that they actually violate or frustrate the accomplishment of the act in a significant way. So taking a payoff for my vote is defined as fraud because it violates in a fundamental way the very meaning of the civic act of voting.

The distinction between an instrumental act like a bank withdrawal and an act that embodies its own purpose, like voting, is an old and venerable one and especially crucial for Aristotle because it gives him the cutting edge for separating out the true community from one that is "in name only" (*Politics* 3.1280b8).[14] We can see this quite clearly if we turn our attention to the specific purpose (or purposes) that could unify citizens into an authentic polity.

Aristotle looks at "mutual defense" as the potential unifying purpose of the state, evidently as popular a notion then as it is now. The word Aristotle employs here—"alliance" or, in the Greek, *summachia*—is particularly suggestive because it connotes a "combining of forces" for protection. One would expect him to note the obvious difficulty in creating a unified public community out of an alliance of diverse forces. But Aristotle's perception is more acute; he notes that alliances, more than being too diverse, actually create too much unity. The "usefulness" of an alliance depends on its ability to employ citizens "who are all alike" (*Politics* 2.1261a26). In defending an alliance, sheer numbers are what count, hence the need to suppress "different kinds" of citizens in favor of the sameness of soldiers ready for battle. If mutual protection were the distinguishing purpose of a civic community, Aristotle notes that "Tyrrhenians and Carthaginians" would then constitute a political community. Updated, that would mean that the United States and all the countries of NATO would be considered, because of their mutual defense pact, a single state![15] While alliances may be appropriate among states, insofar as they are forged *in order to* protect citizens within states, they cannot fully explain the intrinsic purpose of a particular community. These agreements do not account for the

fact that civic communities come together not just in order to protect themselves but for the sake of mutual exchange or what Aristotle calls "reciprocal equivalence" (*to ison to antipeponthos*) (*Politics*
2.1261a31). We will need to unpack that notion, but it should at
least be evident that if individual survival were all that is at stake,
then there would be no need for a constitution (*politeia*). Rather a
simple treaty (*suntheke*) with guaranteed sureties would suffice for
our mutual survival.[16] As the unifying purpose of our public lives,
mutual defense, then, is both too inclusive and too exclusive. It unifies vastly divergent peoples by reducing them all to a single
common denominator—survival. If preserving life is an individual's
goal, community encompasses something more.

That "something more" might be the commercial exchange of
goods. That, too, is a popular modern account of the purpose of
public community, so much so that during the 1980s, with the rapa-
ciousness of Wall Street brokers and the conspicuous consumption
of the wealthy elite, one wonders if business had not become the
sole end "for which governments are instituted among men."
Undoubtedly, we could not survive without commerce, but again it
is Aristotle who puts the marketplace in its proper perspective:
"Even when men do not need the assistance of others, they still
choose to live together" (*Politics* 3.1278b20–22).[17] Like an alliance,
the contract between buyer and seller is at once too encompassing
and too restrictive to account for the phenomenon of the *polis*. We
can trade with almost anyone (even enemies), but trade relations are
hardly sufficient to establish a common polity. In fact, as multi-
national corporations have demonstrated, international trade can
work against the established purposes of a developed country or
undermine the political structure of a developing nation. Obviously,
economic considerations pervade the political agenda in a way Aristotle could never have foreseen. But the limited and instrumental
nature of the buyer-seller relationship remains pretty much
unchanged. A business exchange may well be more multifaceted
than a treaty, but it hardly can approach the richness that seems to
characterize the transactions among citizens. With an Aristotelian
sense for the obvious, overlooked truth, Edmund Burke remarked
that "the state is certainly more than a partnership in pepper and

coffee, calico and tobacco, taken up for a little temporary interest, and to be dissolved by the fancy of the parties."[18]

Certainly, alliances for defense and exchanges of goods do establish a mutuality and hence represent a sharing, but these kinds of sharing, based as they are on a legitimate self-interest, are nevertheless not sufficient to explain the sharing that takes place on the public communal level. Civic life, which involves voting and politicking, is so much richer—at least potentially so. When I vote or, better, participate in a campaign, it hardly makes sense to say I do it in order to survive or for the exchange of commercial goods. Those theoreticians of the minimalist state who legitimize politics only in terms of protection and exchange seem to mistake what Aristotle calls "the necessary conditions" of the polis for politicality itself (*Politics* 3.1280b33).

To ask what politicality is just in itself (as Plato might) or what the intrinsic purposes are that give politics its meaning (as Aristotle might put it) is the next logical step in the vein of exploration we have begun in this chapter. A word of caution, however, is in order. The lodestone over which we stand poised is inexhaustibly rich. The following reflection makes no pretense of an exhaustive or definitive account of the public good. By paying close attention to what it is we do together and the accounts we give to one another of our political transactions, I seek only to uncover those conditions without which the fullness of our shared existence could not be understood.

. . . As Good

"The *polis* is formed not just for the sake of life (*zēn*), but rather, for the sake of the good life (*euzēn*)" (*Politics* 3.1280a32). What Aristotle meant by the "good life" was, of course, not a sizzling steak and a cold beer. Without doing too much violence to the text, we could define the good life, initially at least, as the kind of life that humans recognize *as* good.[19] For Aristotle, the recognition of the moral dimension (the "*as* good") in human acts would have been so obvious as to hardly bear mentioning. For us moderns, for whom the moral dimension is usually seen as some alien grid placed upon acts (usually by an authority figure), it is not at all so self-evident. The modern image of morality in politics is often that of the "religious right" or some such group attempting to impose a self-righteous moral claim upon an unwilling public. That scenario, however forbidding, can deflect us from recognizing an even more important, underlying truth. If we reject the program of the "religious right," it is only because we see it *as* wrong, *as* harmful, *as* an unjustified intrusion into the consciences of citizens. What we may fail to see, then, is that our rejection already assumes a moral stance; indeed, we can only argue our counterclaim within the context of moral discourse. It is because we recognize certain policies *as* good that we reject others *as* evil. When voters vote, when campaigners campaign, even when protesters protest—all are involved in human transactions that inexorably involve the participants for good or ill. These actors may or may not be on a moral crusade, but no accounting of their acts can avoid the fact that what they do and why they do it involves some sense of good either for themselves or others. A few pages back I pointed out how our moral purposes are folded into our acts in such a way as to render those acts incomprehensible without reference to those purposes. Now, perhaps, we can understand why Aristotle almost took for granted the moral character of *logos*: "It is the distinguishing characteristic of humans that they alone, of all animals, are able to recognize good and evil, just and unjust and other moral qualities. And it is the sharing (*koinōnia*) of these recognitions that constitutes a household and a city (*polin*)" (*Politics* 1.1253a17–19).

Any community, then, that is one in more than name only shares a common moral purpose, if only in its most inchoate form— that is, its participants recognize their coming together as something good. There can be, therefore, no such thing as a morally neutral community. If there were, it would surely be a community that was "up to no good"; that is, one that came together for no good purpose.

Of course, that does not mean that every community's purpose thereby *is* good. Whether the community fulfills its purpose and whether its purpose is judged good are questions that are subsequent to the initial moral recognition that every community embodies a purpose which it views *as* good. Law, for example, is a striking instance of our attempt to embody our moral assessments into the very warp and woof of our community. That is why the old bromide "You can't legislate morality" is so misleading. To take it at its face value, such an assertion is patently false. What else could our laws prohibiting murder, rape, and discrimination mean except an embodiment of the community's moral opprobrium? Even if, in a less sweeping sense, the claim is that laws cannot change the habits of citizens, it is still questionable. How else do you explain the considerable transformation of our public language and practices as a result of the civil rights legislation of the 1960s?

Our first assay into the lodestone of our public sharing, then, has afforded us a modest but significant yield. We recognize the sharing of public purposes *as* good; that is, they embody an inescapable moral dimension. Even those purposes we rejected earlier as unworthy of political community—survival and wealth— nonetheless must be understood *as* good (if insufficient) reasons for coming together as citizens.

. . . As the "Mean"

Granting that the "good life" is inherently a moral life, we might ask why a *polis*, or public community, is an appropriate environment for the birth and nurturance of this morally good life. In other words, why is the public community itself recognized *as* good? To answer that question, we must understand what it means when Aristotle calls the *polis* "self-sufficient" (*autarkeia*).[20] And to understand that is to refer back to the ancient wisdom of "the golden mean." Like Goldilocks's third chair, the *polis* is neither too small nor too big— but "just right." While the family community surely displays possibilities for human good—procreation, love, education—it is by its very nature narrowly defined. Indeed, its power comes from the circumscribed intimacy of the relationships. It seeks privacy and shelter from the sometimes harsh glare of public inspection. One of the obvious reasons why the family metaphor does not work in electoral politics is that there are but a few persons (even in the new genetics!) whom we feel comfortable in calling "mother" and "father." Significantly enough, it is usually only in times of political extremity when survival itself is at stake—in war and revolution, for example—that we are tempted to call our fellow citizens "sisters and brothers." Even a community of families or what we call today the extended family does not alter the essential relationships that constitute the family or the authority (whether patriarchal or matriarchal) that organizes those relationships. The Greeks called such a community not a *polis* but an *apoika* (extended home) and its members not *politēs* (citizens) but *homogalactes* (suckled by the same milk). Because both the familial and political communities are established by a mutual sharing, similarities abound, but the temptation to draw too close an analogy between the two must be resisted if we are to be faithful to the specific realities of both orders. What John Courtney Murray calls the "climate of the city" is a "civic amity" which has "nothing to do with the cleavage of a David to a Jonathan, or with the kinship of the clan . . . It is in direct contrast with the passionate fanaticism of the Jacobin: 'Be my brother or I'll kill you.' "[21]

If family relationships are too intimate and too limited to account for the diverse and more remote interchanges among citizens, the entire human community (what the Stoics called the *genus humanum*) on the other hand is too encompassing a reality to generate the specific goods that constitute the good life and to sustain the rich diversity of civic relationships. Certainly, a doctrine of human rights, those moral prescriptions that apply to all humanity, is an absolutely essential part of our living together on a common planet. But the language of rights, with its negative prohibitions (not to be tortured, not to be disenfranchised, etc.) is not sufficient to account for my responsibilities as a citizen in a community. We saw that framing the Bouvia case exclusively as an issue of rights neglected the equally important, perhaps overriding, considerations of the public good.

Some have argued that the threat of a nuclear holocaust compels us to transcend our limited national perspective and see all humanity as one community. The threat of nuclear annihilation is, assuredly, enough motivation to reduce arms and to form alliances even with traditional enemies so that nuclear war may be rendered less imminent. But, as I have already mentioned, treaties formed for our own protection cannot create true communities. In fact, those who argue that nuclear holocaust can be avoided only if we cease to see ourselves as Americans (or Russians for that matter) and adopt a universalist perspective may, unwittingly, be serving their and our cause poorly, so impossible is the condition they demand of us.

At any rate we can see why for the Greeks the *koinōnia politikē* (the political community) was so measured to the *agathon koinon* (the common good). Only in a community that was self-sufficient and hence large enough to provide for the multiplicity of goods that constitute human flourishing—family, friends, art, learning, religion, and politics itself—and yet, at the same time, small enough to allow a participatory interchange among its members, only in that golden mean did the good life become possible.

An obvious objection comes to mind here. The contemporary American republic is far more vast and complex than ancient Athens. Sheer numbers and size would seem to prohibit the application of the Greek "mean" to the modern state. Perhaps. But before we can make that claim we need to look a bit more closely at the character of the relationships that formed the Greek *polis*, at least as Aristotle described it.

Unlike the unalterable hierarchical relationship in the family and the abstract and tenuous bond of the human race, civic relationships involve diverse and fluctuating interactions. Aristotle used the enigmatic phrase already alluded to earlier—*to ison to antipeponthes* (reciprocal equivalence)—to capture the rich and fuller exchange of citizens among themselves as rulers and ruled, representatives and electors, judges and juries, etc.[22] Literally, the phrase means "to suffer what one has inflicted," and, while its political meaning is somewhat in dispute and the text in the *Politics* uncertain, it is clear Aristotle wanted to connote the sense of shared responsibility citizens undertake in the *polis*.[23] So important was this mutual exchange that Aristotle uncharacteristically commends the Athenian religious practice of erecting public shrines to the Graces (*Charites*), whose presence fostered the initiation and return of favors. These exchanges, regulated by the preeminent political principle and virtue, justice, were, for Aristotle, the glue that binds a community together, and they alone were capable of "saving the city" (*Nichomachean Ethics* 5.1133a1–5).

In Athens, then a city of ten thousand citizens, it was hardly possible nor necessary that each citizen come to know every other citizen. A political community was constituted instead by those mutual exchanges established by the *politeia* (the constitution) and the laws which expressed the common purposes of the citizens. The criticism that the United States has too many people to establish a civic identity in the Greek sense might have some force, but I suspect it too often misses the point because it views the Greek *polis* as a place where everyone knew one another. While the United States is undeniably larger than the Athenian *polis*, it may still be possible to experience here that reciprocity Aristotle talks about, particularly if we can articulate and live out our shared purposes. One might even add that the media, in spite of its obvious limitations, could help foster a common reciprocity unknown even in Aristotle's day. At any rate, the quality of our reciprocal exchanges is clearly a much more important issue and its debate inherently more fruitful than the quarrel about numbers and square miles.

. . . As "Natural"

If political life is analogous to Goldilocks's chair, then it must provide for us in a way that neither the family nor humanity as a whole can. To look for the specific purposes that only a political community serves is to raise the age-old question of what constitutes the public good. Whatever its content and however much it may vary from place to place and time to time, the public good is what gives politics its unique identity. Political sharing is unlike any other sharing because it provides for human goods which the intimate familial sharing or the universal sharing of a common humanity cannot. Edmund Burke offered a particularly evocative account of that specifically political good when he described it as "a partnership in all science, a partnership in all art, a partnership in every virtue and in all perfection . . . a partnership . . . between those who are living, those who are dead and those who are to be born."[24]

It would be impossible to imagine a culture, much less a civilization, existing without the nurturance of a political order of some kind. One need not endorse the full sweep of Burke's vision yet still agree that politics encompasses much more than the instrumental function of protection and commerce. As we have already seen, the public good is inherently a moral good that goes beyond but does not exclude mere survival and economic transaction. "The common good," as Maritain puts it, "is not only a system of advantages and utilities but also a rectitude of life, an end, good in itself . . . a *bonum honestum*.[25] It is also, as Burke suggests, a historical good; that is, the communal ties encompass a sense of time and place, of history and geography, that much like the diachronic and synchronic notes of a musical scale play a tune infinitely more rich than the timeless, spaceless individual of the social contract tradition. The articulation of that public good, one of the essential functions of public philosophy, involves not the construction of a moral overlay to an already constituted community but rather the teasing out (and even critique) of those goods already inherent in the purposes that bring humans together. So . . . "to form a more perfect union, establish justice, insure domestic tranquility, provide for the common defense, promote the general welfare and secure the blessings of liberty to ourselves and our posterity" are purposes discovered in the very exigencies of living together when that living together seeks a more diverse and richer reciprocity than either a family or humankind as a whole could sustain.

Only within this context, perhaps, do we dare utter the all too familiar but profound phrase of Aristotle's that we are "by nature political beings" (*phusei politikon zōon*) (*Politics* 1.1253a3). "Nature" here does not mean "instinct" or "not subject to choice" for it is possible *to survive* without a *polis* and the Greeks had no dearth of examples either in literature (the Cyclopes) or in real life (the barbarians). Rather, it means that those excellences (*aretai*) which constitute the good life (*euzēn*)—art, play, learning, to name but a few—can only emerge and flourish within a community chosen and established for those purposes.[26] To deny someone the opportunity to share in a political community is to deny her or him the possibility of a life of excellence (*aretē*), of happiness (*eudaimonia*), and of noble acts (*praxeōn kalōn*) (*Politics* 3.1281a2–3). Just as surely as "the unexamined life is not worth living" because, as Socrates saw, it violates our very humanity *not* to think, so the prohibition of political freedom would also be a denial of our humanity. In such a view, slavery and the disenfranchisement of women are evils not just because they violate the rights of individual human beings but also because they truncate our shared, common nature. "Outside a *polis*," ring Aristotle's immortal words, a person is either "a beast or a god." Like the denial of birth and death mentioned earlier, the denial of our political nature is equally self-defeating because only in the fullest sharing made possible by a political community can the self find the fullest development of its nature. To walk away from our public community is to walk away from ourselves, to diminish ourselves. That is why Stephen Tonsor remarked:

> The question is not whether or not one has a right to withdraw from society, to make the great refusal, to break the bonds which bind men together for purposes of mutual fulfillment; the question is not whether we shall be political or not, but, rather, how we shall be political and what the ends of our politics shall be.[27]

Given the inescapability of the political and the good inherent in all our public transactions, the debate whether or not the public good is universal and absolute seems barren and abstract. That there is a public good, that it can be more or less articulated, that there are standards inherent in the meaning of our acts—all this seems evident if one pays close attention to what we do and what we say. Even the staunchest pluralist today would not argue that genocide is one of the many goods a community might wish to affirm, and even the most rigorous advocate of a natural law theory of the good would not claim that there is a definitive, unalterable and timeless list of public goods.[28] We can distinguish between choosing something (say, representative government) *as* good and saying that our choosing it makes it good. What we choose as goods are not thereby arbitrary goods, but that does not foreclose the possibility of an inventive and creative choosing that reveals previously undiscovered aspects of the good. It is possible certainly to recognize the unique and unpredictable nature of political communities without claiming that the source of that uniqueness is the arbitrary nature of the goods they choose. So, for example, we understand why the founders of the American republic could not and did not announce universal health care as a public good but why we their successors might accept that challenge today. We also understand, given the nature of our democracy, why voting fraud then and now must be treated as criminal. This is one of the responsibilities of a public philosophy: employing practical wisdom to discern the specific public good for this polity at this time and in this place. That would not be necessary if the public good were to be logically deduced from a changeless principle according to invariant rules, and it would not be possible if the public good were defined however a community wanted to define it. In the former, politics is reduced to a technological activity that destroys the citizens' capacity to participate and judge; in the latter it is transformed into an instrumental activity whose modus operandi is manipulation and propaganda. Given the history of modern politics, we can appreciate Aristotle's reminder about how difficult it is to hit the mean.

We might be able to get a better fix on the natural, even pervasive way the political informs our lives if we look briefly at the different senses of "politics" and the "good" toward which it aims.

1. "Politics," in its specific sense, characterizes the public exchange of citizens *as* citizens. In common endeavors and in public argument, the goals, character, and policies of the civic community are established and carried out. As such, politics constitutes a distinctive way of acting and speaking that marks it off from other endeavors such as art, education, and sport. Yet, like these activities, politics is engaged in for its own sake; ulterior purposes, as we have already noted, have a way of distorting, even violating the intrinsic meaning of political speech and action. What citizens seek to embody in their common endeavors the founders of the American republic called the "public good," and the enjoyment of that enterprise they named "public happiness."[29]

2. Inasmuch as the good of the community as a whole involves more than just "politicking," there is a second, more encompassing

meaning of "politics." Because citizens are responsible for the health, commerce, education, leisure, art, and even the religion of their *polis*, the agenda of politics involves in some sense the ordering of these activities within the community. So, this second sense of politics might be called the "political order." This all-encompassing *telos* (end) of the political order is what the Greeks called the *koinon agathon* (the common good). Since no other community could claim such an embracing responsibility, Aristotle thought of politics in this sense as the highest and noblest human activity.

3. Although Aristotle does not mention it, there is a third sense of politics which characterizes the "political dimension" embedded in activities not specifically political (that is, in meaning #1). In this sense, politics is not an all-embracing (meaning #2) phenomenon but it is a pervasive, if inferior, dimension of all our shared transactions. Because of the mutuality inherent in any type of community, it is not surprising that attention is paid to the politics of family, the politics of academia, the politics of church and synagogue. It is perhaps in this sense that politics is an inescapable reality. We may choose to forgo political involvement in the affairs of government, but how could we avoid altogether the political dimension of familial or academic life? The great danger here is that the political dimension might overwhelm the activity of which it is but a part. When that happens, we speak of an organization or an event as becoming "overly politicized." The decade of the sixties in America was certainly a time when our awareness of and involvement in the political dimension of almost everything was most acute, perhaps overly so. In pulling back from that extreme, however, we cannot forget that it is in this third sense of politics that we most often receive our first schooling in the possibilities of "public happiness."

Much more could be said—indeed, needs to be said—about these various senses of politics.[30] For now, I want only to point out that such a preliminary assay reveals how distinctive, how encompassing, how utterly pervasive the phenomenon of politics is. It is the element in which we live, move, and have our being: in short, our nature. To treat our shared public existence as if it were merely an instrumental good, a mere means to some private end, some private happiness, would be to shear off its richness, violate its integrity, pervert it into something it is not. To treat political activity as "political action committees" (PACs) might do, as the means whereby some private interest is protected, sets a dangerous precedent not just because the interest itself might be suspect (for example, the "right" to own a machine gun) but also because the public good becomes lost and no one can be found to be responsible for it.

"All well and good," a sympathetic critic might rejoin, "but it is possible to give too much weight to the political. Your spirited defense of the political is in danger of overreaching itself. Who among us today would claim with Aristotle that politics is the highest and noblest activity? It is that second meaning of politics that is so problematic; no matter how fitting it might have been for the largely homogeneous Greek *polis*, any attempt to impose normative common goods upon reluctant individuals in a pluralist democracy surely courts disaster." In the face of such criticism the more prudent route for public philosophy to take would seem to be to stress the distinctive nature of the political (meaning #1) with some passing reference to and cautionary comments upon the political dimension in other activities (meaning #3) . . . and leave it at that. Even without the more ambitious meaning (#2), politics could nonetheless recoup its place *among* (if not above) other worthy human endeavors.

The problem with such a strategy is that it ignores what is sometimes an unwelcome truth about our lives: their dependence on a public political order. In a very real sense, although we must be extremely careful how we define that sense, all aspects of our existence, even our most closely held moral and religious beliefs, are at the mercy of a political order which has the power to foster or inhibit them. If we doubt that, we need but remember Elizabeth Bouvia. Her very private decision to quit her life necessitated the permission or interdiction of the court. And even if we judge that requirement an unnecessary intrusion of the judicial order into our lives, that judgment itself is a political decision which some branch of government must endorse if, for example, the so-called right to die is to be recognized.

Religious practice provides an even more striking example. By recognizing that religious liberty is a fundamental and perhaps even the "first liberty" in our polity, the political order sanctions its exercise. Yet it also checks and orders it to some extent. So, to maim, torture, or sacrifice another in the name of a religious obligation is forbidden. It matters not that the victim is a consenting party to the sacrifice. God transcends the political order, of that no believer doubts; but, strangely enough, it is the political order which assigns the place religious practice is to occupy in the public domain. In a theocracy, of course, that would not be the case; there the political order would be subservient to the shared purposes that have brought the community of believers together. Here, religious freedom emerges from the soil of our political commitments.

It is important that I not be misunderstood here. I am not saying that politics should exercise a hegemony over family life, art, education, and the like; rather, I am only pointing out that unlike these latter activities which make no pretense at ordering for the whole community, politics does. Actually, it is by recognizing the encompassing order of the political that we are better able, I believe, to resist its hegemonic tendencies.

Ultimately, then, there is no more awesome responsibility than citizenship and for that reason no nobler activity. The citizen is responsible for everything in the life of the community but in a very subtle way. The citizen cannot ignore the call to order rightly the republic; at the same time he or she must guard the integrity of every good activity within the republic. The citizens' responsibility today, perhaps more so than in Aristotle's time, is to see that this awesome political power (in Michael Walzer's words) "be sustained and that it be inhibited."[31] Hence, the political order more often than not will regulate at the boundaries of, rather than within, the various other communal goods. This is undoubtedly a profound tension, one that can only be approached with a good deal of prudence. There is no calculus for its resolution, but in each issue (like the Bouvia case) it must be faced anew and in each generation confronted anew. Is it any wonder, then, so terrifying and so necessary is this task, that the Greeks thought of piety—the approach toward the sacred in fear and trembling—as an essential political virtue?

. . . As Transformative

We have, admittedly, traveled a long way from the specific policy issues of the Elizabeth Bouvia case. Our purpose, however, has been rather steadfast: to mine the sense of good that lies embedded in our public transactions. That broad and pervasive communal good meets us at every turn, at home and at work, at social gatherings and athletic contests. It greets us even at the synagogue and church doors. Wherever we gather for a common purpose, the public good is there.

However, we need to sift through the rich vein of those public transactions one more time to see if we can locate a specific one that embodies the characteristic quality of our distinctively political acts. That lodestone has been with us all along, since the very beginnings of our investigation: it is the law. What first captured our attention was, after all, Bouvia's appeal to the law to resolve the conflicting demands of private right and the public good. Later, we noted how the law captured in a concrete way our moral purposes. And now we shall find in the law no more striking example of the power politics possesses to transform our private transactions into public significance.

To make the point, let me turn to a very prosaic example: a young couple contemplating marriage. For the sake of argument, I will assume they have been living together for some time and have already made certain promises of fidelity to each other. Why get married? Indeed, they assume they already are "married" and except for certain relatively minor inconvenient legal and economic sanctions, who needs the "piece of paper"? (Forgive the anachronistic, 1960-ish cast of the argument. It suits my purposes and I rather doubt the reasons why 1990s couples marry are any clearer than why 1960s couples didn't!) Certainly, a legal or even religious ceremony cannot undo the moral relationship already established, no matter how much society might disapprove. Rightly or wrongly, their living together implies shared purposes and a moral transaction. "Laws," as Robert Sokolowski puts it, "are not the first insertion of a common human life."[32] But they are a "further actualization," and by that phrase Robert Sokolowski means the relationship becomes refined, clarified, more sharply articulated, even amplified. In a civil and religious ceremony the couple's relationship is sanctioned. The couple's purposes and commitments become instances of a larger public purpose. The marriage laws comprehend the couple in a way their own moral purposes cannot, and in that comprehension the goods of marriage and family are proclaimed, protected, nurtured. The eyes of the law sometimes see further than the shortsighted view of the lovers, and the arms of the law reach further than their intimate embrace. It's hard to imagine a society which did not in some way sanction some form of marriage; but, lest marriage laws too easily be interpreted as a disguised instrument of social control, imagine a family attempting to live out its common purpose in a society totally hostile to its good. Socrates' example in the *Republic* of the sharing of wives and children represents a literary monition; Russia briefly after the 1917 Revolution a historical one. The couple's new identity, their new public face in marriage is then both a submission and a transformation. They submit their personal commitment to a regulative civil order which in turn sanctions, perhaps even sanctifies, their mutual pledges. They are now no longer living together but married with a new public identity. It is, for that reason, not a "state to be entered into lightly," not a vow to be pledged capriciously. Their promises are not just personal but civic.

It is those same vows that capture so dramatically the character of marriage, that "most personal and yet most public transaction" (again Robert Sokolowski's words).[33] The words "I James take you Helen . . ." with the reiterative third person represent no mere ornamental overlay but rather, as Robert Sokolowski puts it, a "laminated statement" that captures both the personal and the public nature of the marriage vow. In the "I take you" the couple initiates the moral transaction, thereby creating a new status for themselves as moral agents. In the "James takes Helen" the couple use their public names and thereby allow their mutual pledging to be taken up into a legal, civic purpose. The act whereby they become husband and wife enters the public record, altering their status as citizens. Marriage is not a rebirth, but it is a new beginning that has significant import for the whole community. In a real sense, the marriage ceremony represents a dual act of trust: the couple who choose to live their life together believe that society will nurture and foster their relationship, and the state (by sanctioning their union) affirms its trust in the couple to assume their responsibilities as a family within the civic community. Given the significant erosion of public trust in the 1960s, it is not surprising then that couples expressed cynicism about the institution of marriage.

While marriage is a particularly appropriate example because it captures the transformation from private to public status, the political arena is replete with examples of such illuminating laminated statements as: "I, William Jefferson Clinton, do solemnly swear to uphold the Constitution of these United States . . ." Or when a jury representing the civic community renders judgment on a violation of the law: "We the jury find the defendant guilty." And, perhaps, the political paradigm of all such personal and public pledges: "We, the people of the United States, in order to form a more perfect union . . . do ordain and establish this Constitution."

With these words a new political order (*e pluribus unum*) was enunciated and a new relationship among the citizens, a "second life" to borrow Arendt's phrase, was established—one, we might mention, that transcended not only their personal, social, and business relationships but even prior political engagements.[34] For good or ill, the Constitution defines us, as United States citizens, in a way that no other characterizations—friend, lover, husband, or parent—can. To disclaim that identity or to count it as naught or even to assess its significance far below my other identities (as friend and lover, for example) is itself to perform a political act predicated upon an identity I now reject or discount. More specifically, there is a sense in which I cannot dismiss the rule of law in the same way I can dismiss the social or moral censure of my neighbors. A black in the South in the 1950s could perhaps dismiss or skirt racist attitudes in a way that he could not ignore racist institutions sanctioned by law. A polity, including ours, determines the public forms of relationships, defines what is to count as crime and violation, regulates the obligations of parents and children, establishes the type of education, and so much more.[35] It was this understanding of polity that Plato had in mind when, in the *Crito*, the Laws confront Socrates in his cell and remind him that it was they who provided for his birth, his education, his marriage, and even promoted his vocation as a philosopher. It is then this sense of polity and law that embodies our shared purposes, our *koinōnia*. Law transforms our fragile moral assessments into enduring community commitments, thereby making possible a concrete yet abiding sense of the common good.[36]

Perhaps an example might be helpful here. Let us take the leering advances of an executive toward his female secretary. His sexual innuendos, verbal badgering, and even not-so-subtle hints that her advancement entails the granting of certain "favors" are all morally offensive. But the moral situation affords the secretary few alternatives; she can submit to the offensive behavior or quit her job and lose financial security, or she may strike back in what could be a futile or even dangerous gesture. If, however, this behavior is captured by the legal assessment of "sexual harassment," the individual moral struggle becomes a community concern, and nonviolent vindication at least becomes possible. The issue is defined no longer as one woman's objection to offensive behavior—behavior which the executive may very well claim is not objectionable—but now as a community assessment, embodied in the law prohibiting sexual harassment in the workplace, it becomes part of the public good which the community is willing to advocate and enforce. What makes this a particularly interesting example is that such laws are often advocated by the very same liberals who decry efforts to legislate morality. Even more fascinating (though well beyond our purview here) is the meaning of sexual conduct implicit in such laws. It would seem to be in conflict with the prevailing mores, for how can sex mean whatever you want it to mean (a popular view) and still be defined in very specific cases as harassment? After all, if companies can require grumbling employees to conform to dress codes, why can they not require them to put up with sexually obnoxious and demanding executives? Unless, of course, there are important intrinsic differences in the very meaning of dress codes and sexual conduct. Be that as it may, if prohibitions against sexual harassment are not arbitrary coercions put upon us by overly prudish women (and I think they are not), then they have to represent the community's assessment about just relationships in our society.

That laws will, at times, fail to embody the appropriate moral commitments or merely become, in the hands of a ruler or class, instruments of social control cannot be gainsaid. My only point is that unless laws are seen as a comprehension of what is good, not merely as coercion, no rational criterion will exist to criticize bad laws or the misuse of law by a privileged class.

> Because of this, political struggles are never merely matters of self interest, never merely attempts to get at the public trough; at their most acute they are struggles to make an assessment prevail, to capture the soul of a society, to share the transactions and relationships that will predominate.[37]

Robert Sokolowski's words seem particularly applicable here, for what else was Elizabeth Bouvia attempting to do (particularly in her first suit) but to "make her assessment prevail" in a way that would shape society's relationship with those who wished to commit suicide. Judge Hews's verdict, "This society values life," represented the already prevailing counterassessment. As I mentioned earlier, this first case was not a traditional "rights" case—Ms. Bouvia certainly had the right to withdraw from the hospital; rather, she wanted us to agree with her assessment about the uselessness of her life and so, in this case at least, define our relationship with her and our obligations toward her based on that assessment.

"We are a people of laws, not men," or so we like to characterize ourselves. Even at its most acrimonious level, legal disputes like Ms. Bouvia's are still to be preferred to the rejection of the rule of law, sometimes mistakenly referred to as "the taking of law into one's own hands." By taking the law into our own partisan hands we destroy it and end up no different than the one-eyed Cyclops: "No public place of adjudication have they, no laws; rather they live on the tops of lofty mountains, in hollow caves, laying down the law to wife and children with no care for anyone else" (*Odyssey* 9.112–115).

We need only to look at the Charles Bronson *Death Wish* saga or recall Bernard Goetz acting out in the real world his vengeful fantasy to see how close we remain in imagination to Homer's Cyclops. In the overly litigious society we have created, in which the guilty do seem all too often to go unpunished, it is so easy to forget the lesson Aeschylus tried to teach the equally impatient Athenians. In the *Oresteia*, where retribution piles upon retribution, where revenge calls out for even greater revenge, the triumph of civilization is represented by Athena's taking the matter out of the blood-stained hands of the partisans and assigning responsibility for its resolution to the impartial judgment of a jury.[38]

Equally eloquent as Aeschylus's *Oresteia* on the transformative power of law is Plato's final great work, the *Laws*. In that masterpiece, the old philosopher who once espoused the rule of the philosopher-king now argues that rulers are but "servants of the law." In a marvelous extended word play he retells the story of Chronos, who, recognizing that humans could not rule their own affairs without succumbing to pride (*hubris*) and injustice (*adikos*), appointed a godly race (*daimons*) to rule the affairs of men. We too, the old Athenian argues, should follow that tradition in rule over our homes and cities by obeying the divine element (*daimonos*) in us; that is, the dispensation (*dianomos*) of reason (*nous*) which is named (*epenomozō*) law (*nomos*). True law (*orthos nomos*), rather than representing the interest of the establishment (Thrasymachus's old definition in the *Republic*), expresses an inviolable sacred order because it is oriented toward the good of the community. On this point, more than anything else, Plato concludes, rests the "salvation of the *polis*."[39]

Our phenomenological excavation has sought to legitimate the notion of public good by locating it not outside but within the fabric of our mutual interactions. Those actions as embodiments of human purposes contain within them possibilities for good or ill, possibilities which either call forth or frustrate the fulfillment of those purposes. As surely as the meaning inherent in the marriage covenant contains within it the possibilities for fidelity and betrayal, so citizenship embodies mutual purposes such that patriotism and treason represent possibilities waiting to be actualized. In sum, the public good is woven into the very warp and woof of our civic life.

Recognizing the legitimate, even the indispensable role that the public good plays in human affairs, however, does not tell us how to go about resolving all the thorny issues citizens confront in their public transactions. We have unearthed a principle that can guide us, not a calculus that resolves everything. Though the public good can never mean whatever we *want* it to mean, what it does mean will have to be articulated in every polity and in every age. What the public good is and ought to be for twenty-first-century Americans will be a task that must be confronted by us and by those that follow. How the public good relates to that other polar star in the American firmament—private rights—must continually be worked out, always with a certain mixture of vigor and caution. Helping citizens to think those issues through is undoubtedly the vocation of the public philosopher.

Elizabeth Bouvia Redux

With that in mind, let us take a second look at the Elizabeth Bouvia case—this time through the corrective lens of the public good—in order to determine whether or not we can see any clearer through the dense fog of issues that her court litigations present. I alluded in the previous chapter to the possibility that the two court decisions might represent a prudential balance between the competing claims of the public good and private right. In the first case, the claim of the public good, namely the state's interest in protecting innocent human life, is balanced, in the second case, by the court's protection of a citizen's right to refuse unwanted medical treatment. I doubt that such a balance was merely serendipitous; rather it is the fruit of a deeply embedded, historical constitutional tradition. The practical wisdom of those decisions might better be distilled if, again, we look at each one separately.

Had Elizabeth Bouvia been successful in securing a state-assisted suicide—"the ultimate exercise of one's right to privacy," as the court duly noted—one wonders what goods if any might then be designated as "public."[40] When Judge Hews appealed to the good of preserving life, he sought, I believe, to check that dangerous imbalance. He did that by first of all asserting, at least implicitly, that there is a legitimate public-good consideration at stake here.[41] Secondly, he instantiated the formal notion of a public good by appealing to the age-old prohibition against taking innocent life.

Thirdly, and most controversially, he determined that the inviolable good of innocent life overrides other goods such as individual desire and perceived quality of life. We might better appreciate the import of the judge's decision by attending to some alternate courses of action he chose not to take.

Had Judge Hews found in favor of the plaintiff, the obvious question would follow: On what possible grounds could the state mandate cooperation in a citizen's suicide? Because she wants it? That is patently absurd. Even if what she wanted would not violate others' consciences (as it inevitably would), we could still object that a state whose purpose was to serve the whims of its citizens without presuming to judge the public good or evil of those wishes would surely be emasculated. At the mercy of countless Antigones, the emaciated state would be rendered powerless to protect the very individuals for whom it was created. That fear may seem overstated until one realizes that for every one Elizabeth Bouvia there may well be hundreds of individuals (not to mention corporations) who would stop at nothing to satiate their greed at the public's expense.[42] The ethicist Daniel Callahan has argued rather persuasively that we have come perilously close to such a condition, evidenced by our willingness today to "forswear communal goods" and replace "ultimate ends with procedural safeguards."[43] The upshot is a public ethic that Callahan calls "minimalist," in the sense that, while we will not violate others' rights, neither will we be inclined to civic involvement and mutual support. Much earlier, in 1960, John Courtney Murray warned against the reliance on this procedural consensus: "No society in history has ever achieved and maintained an identity and rigor in action unless it has had some substance, unless it has been sustained and directed by some body of substantive beliefs."[44] Both these public philosophers attest to an age-old wisdom that goes back at least as far as Plato: "A true political art cares, of necessity, not for private interest but the common good; for the common good binds together a *polis*; private interest tears it asunder" (*Laws* 9.875). Without some shared body of beliefs, procedural safeguards operate in a vacuum. At best, a republic that has no substantive commitments but only procedural safeguards forms an Aristotelian alliance, established for the sole purpose of protecting the security of supposedly autonomous individuals. At worst, such a polity eventually commits "policide" by starving itself to feed the insatiable appetites of individual citizens. In the Bouvia case at least, something more than procedural safeguards was affirmed: the public good of a citizen's life. As Judge Hews ruled, "society's interest in preserving life . . . outweighed her right to self-determination."[45]

If the priority of life over self-determination were to be reversed, Bouvia would have to offer more than just an affirmation of her right to do as she pleased. The reason why she believed the presumption in favor of life could be overruled here was that the quality of her life had deteriorated to the point where continuing in life was pointless. She wanted the court (and, by extension, all of us) to share that assessment or, at the very least, to grant that her own assessment was rational. That assessment does in fact seem to be shared by some justices in the second (1986) appellate case. Not content simply to affirm Bouvia's right to refuse the nasogastric tube (absent any clear intent upon suicide), the court, in the majority opinion, further speculated that "the quality of her life has been diminished to the point of helplessness, uselessness, unenjoyability and frustration." Because she would be subject to "ignominy, embarrassment, humiliation and dehumanization" as a result of having to be "fed, cleaned, turned, bedded, toileted by others," the court concluded that Ms. Bouvia's "life has been physically destroyed and its quality, dignity and purpose gone." In a concurring opinion, Judge Compton took that assessment to its fateful conclusion; he argued, in flat opposition to Judge Hews, that we should "be assisting her to die with ease and dignity."[46]

I could not treat here in any exhaustive way the extensive and often convoluted argument over quality versus sanctity of life. Nor do I need to. The thrust of this chapter has been to argue *that there is* a public good, not to develop ways for resolving competing claims about conflicting goods. Since the earlier Bouvia case pushed the issue of individual rights to the extreme end of reducing the state to a mere facilitator of private interest, my argument attempts to address that imbalance and thus clearly supports Judge Hews's argument that the protection of innocent human life (a substantive public good) might legitimately override, in this case at least, a private wish to have an assisted suicide. There are, of course, other public goods, and "quality of life" may well be one of them. If so, two points need to be made. First of all, if "quality of life" is not just to be a code phrase for private interest—that is, if quality of life is truly a *standard* (as the judges quoted above seem to imply)—then it cannot mean whatever a citizen wants it to mean. Those who argue that such a standard should replace the traditional inviolability of innocent human life are struggling (to hearken back to Robert Sokolowski's phrase) "to make an assessment prevail." What is at stake in their efforts "to capture the soul of a society" is not individual rights but what is to count as ultimately good.[47] Secondly, the quality-of-life standard is not inherently inconsistent with nor need it be in conflict with the protection of life. Insofar as "quality of life" stands for the flourishing of human life, it is certainly a notion consistent with my own argument that survival alone cannot serve as a sufficient purpose for political community. In its broadest sense the phrase "quality of life" might simply echo the colonial ideal of the "pursuit of happiness" and, as such, can hardly be construed as inconsistent with the other rights of life and liberty proclaimed in the Declaration of Independence.

Unfortunately, in the Bouvia case the quality-of-life standard means something very specific, and it does clash with the more traditional right-to-life standard. To apply it as the concurring judge in the later (1986) case does is to claim that innocent human life may be taken by the state when such a life is judged to fall short of a standard that would define a tolerable life: that is, a life without the physical deterioration and mental embarrassments that characterize a debilitating disease like cerebral palsy. Because I find that so ominous a prospect, I would like to digress a bit and reflect on the moral and political implications of substituting this new quality-of-life standard for the traditional proscription against taking innocent life.[48]

Even to the very liberal palate, a state-assisted killing warranted by a quality-of-life standard has got to be hard to swallow. We are asked to share an altogether questionable assessment about the intolerable quality of life sufferers of cerebral palsy endure and then, granting that, we are required to assist in the suicide of a patient who has not been characterized in any medical or legal sense as dying. One would think that our experience with totalitarianism and its elimination of the unfit would be sufficient inhibition from even considering such a course of action. Certainly, there is no constitutional nor legal precedent in this country for the killing of innocent patients no matter what the quality of life. So-called right-to-die cases, such as Karen Ann Quinlan and even Nancy Cruzan, are almost always about the right to forgo medical treatment when it is deemed inefficacious and heavily burdensome to the patient.[49] These precedents have not condoned suicide, much less state-supported active euthanasia.

The fact that the quality-of-life standard would operate and the subsequent killing would be permitted only if the patient consented—that I find no more comforting than permitting voluntary servitude. Slavery is forbidden regardless of the slave's willingness to consent because the practice itself is destructive of our humanity and the very meaning of citizenship. The state protects innocent life not because individuals happen to value it but because, like art and learning and community itself, it is recognized by citizens *as* good. As we noted earlier in this chapter, moral categories are not arbitrary judgments superimposed upon physical acts; rather, they are embedded in the very meaning of human transactions. Rights, as we saw, are not political constructions but flow from the nonarbitrary nature of human goods, and so if life is an inalienable right, then we can hardly condone the taking of life even if, as in this case, the patient wants to be killed. The problems with the quality-of-life standard as defined in the Bouvia case become evident when we consider how it might be applied. If applied universally and unconditionally (that is, consent notwithstanding) it would be viewed rightly as a moral abomination. If applied conditionally (that is, with consent as a precondition) it not only relativizes itself but everything else in its wake, including the state's obligation to protect innocent human life.

In invoking the constitutional tradition of the inherent good or, if you will, the sacredness of life, Judge Hews followed, I believe, the wiser course. It was not their recognition of a certain quality of life that led the founders of the republic to proclaim the inalienable right to life but simply the value of life itself. The issue here is not whether a certain qualitative enhancement of one's life is a good worth seeking; indeed it is. Rather, the question is whether the civic community ought to take innocent life when the quality of that life, invariably defined in an arbitrary fashion, dips below an accepted standard. I cannot imagine a more ominous and dangerous precedent, a precedent which fortunately Judge Hews did not establish. There is a profound and perhaps tragic irony in all of this: by demanding her autonomy this modern-day Antigone has forced us to affirm the public good; by claiming the uselessness of her life, she forced us to acknowledge the good of every life, including her own.

In the decade of the nineties, the partisans of individual rights have shifted the debate to a plane more conclusive to their position. Instead of demanding state cooperation they seek to restrict government interference. To allow but not mandate physician-assisted suicide would seem to strike a better balance between individual rights and the public good. Perhaps. But the arguments will have to address not only numerous practical problems such a policy would entail but the very real public assessment that it embodies: namely, that the individual desire to end one's life will, in certain situations at least, not be forestalled by the public obligation to protect innocent human life.[50] No matter how understandable the reasons, the legalization of the direct and intentional killing of innocent patients presents profound difficulties not just for the medical profession's ethic of preserving life but for the entire republic that espouses the inalienable right to life.

In my argument thus far I have sought to restore a lost balance in the American polity. The first Bouvia case brings home the dreadful consequences that the neglect of the public good can lead us into. I have sought to ground the claim of the public good, to give it a legitimacy, in a way that any citizen, independent of his or her political persuasion, might understand. However, I noted in chapter 1 that the real genius of the American experiment was its balancing of those two polar claims: the public good and private interest. So a note of caution needs to be added here lest we forget the claim of individual self-determination and become a Creon to our modern Antigone. The second Bouvia case is a potent reminder of how far some people, here medical professionals, are willing to go to impose their notion of what is good on a reluctant individual. The high-handed management of Elizabeth Bouvia's case at High Desert Hospital bears witness to a liberal society's greatest fear: in the name of a public good, individual rights will be violated by an administrative elite. If we are to avoid that *querelle des anciens et des modernes*, we must tack ever so carefully between the ancients' prescription for a wisdom that discerns the public good and the moderns' insistence on a consent that recognizes the freedom of self-determination. Undoubtedly, representative government requires citizens' consent if it is to be legitimate. (Of course, that consent does not mean a citizen must agree with every decision of the government but, rather, that the form and structure of government exist by virtue of the consent of the governed.) Even so, that consent, while necessary, is hardly sufficient to legitimate a polity. What legitimates a state is not just that the citizens want something (say, protection or fine arts) but that what they want is seen *as good*. Otherwise, a state might be "merely an organ, or an expression, of collective selfishness" and thus, as Leo Strauss notes, no different than a "gang of robbers."[51] The public good that a people consent to could hardly be arbitrarily chosen if it is to be legitimate. Elsewise, why not consent to racism, sexism, and whatever perversion attracts the citizenry? No, protection and fine arts, like all goods, are desired because they are good, not good because they are desired. As Grisez and Boyle remark, the Declaration of Independence does not say that people *want* "life, liberty and the pursuit of happiness," but it declares we have a *right* to those goods.[52]

Now, consent itself is a good. "Cities do not grow like plants," and what Leo Strauss meant by that remark is that cities are human phenomena and so embody choice and action. It is, then, a legitimate concern when Elizabeth Bouvia's consent is continually violated, even if what she wanted was something the public consensus disallows—suicide. No reasonable person would consent to a government that systematically violated her freedom. And there's the rub. If the balance has in the more recent past swung too far in favor of individual consent, it is not impossible that corrective efforts might err in the opposite direction. For that reason one should applaud the resolution of the second court battle that allowed Ms. Bouvia to refuse the hospital's dietary regimen. Despite the Superior Court's obfuscation of the issue by introducing the quality-of-life standard, its decision to halt the manipulative schemes of the staff who forced Ms. Bouvia to barter for pain medication served to protect her dignity. Even if one questioned Ms. Bouvia's caloric intake, persuasive efforts to get her to eat more would clearly have been the wiser course.

The key here, obviously, is how one balances private right and the public good. I do not think there is, nor can there be, a calculus for working out that balance. A practical wisdom that is finely tuned to the distinct nature and history of the American polity must determine in each situation what is the right course of action. My own efforts on behalf of the public good have to be understood as a corrective to the prevailing winds of individual rights. A fuller account would entail a phenomenology of rights that emerges from the legitimating context of our moral transactions. Though the clamor for rights can at times become silly—in one campus newspaper I was amused to discover a heretofore unknown right, the "right of students to drink in a relaxed, laid-back atmosphere"—that is not the problem. What makes calls for rights fractious and disruptive is that they often are not grounded in a substantive notion of community.[53] Yet if we paid close attention to our shared existence it would become clear, I think, that there can be no community without real individuals and no uniqueness without authentic community. In criticizing the community of Plato's *Republic* for its effacement of difference and its misguided goal of sameness, Aristotle makes this remarkable statement: "There are two causes, more than any others, that create a bond of friendship among men: a sense of my own (*idion*) and a sense of affection (*agapēton*)" (*Politics* 2.1262b23). He is thinking here, in contrast to Plato's sharing of wives and children, of the affection we hold for our own children, and what is so noteworthy in this champion of community is that he senses there can be no real sharing without a sense of self and what is "my own."

Perhaps an image might help to order the diverse relationships encountered in the modern *polis*. Imagine a well-constructed and

artfully arranged mansion, Jeffersonian if you like. Our phenomenological excavations into the nature of our public transactions have
provided the foundation for the *polis*. The strong supporting beams
located and exposed in the basement constitute the human rights
upon which community must build. The first floor encompasses all
those political rights and obligations that form the heart of our
shared existence. The other floors and rooms, which vary according
to the resources of the community, represent the diverse activities
and reciprocal sharing that occupy our lives together, from our
business transactions to leisure enjoyments. The laws form the
architecture of the house, dividing the floors, arranging the rooms.
At the top, there must be a skylight open to the sun and stars, the
illuminated and mysterious divine element of which Plato spoke. Of
course, this is but a weak analogy, a mere hint of the direction we
must follow should we offer a full-blown account of the public
good. Here it is sufficient to remark that the two separate court
decisions—the first establishing the overriding public good of preserving innocent life and the second preserving individual liberty in
the face of institutional assaults—at least come close to striking that
balance Madison himself seemed to have in mind.

Elizabeth Bouvia's return to the Los Angeles/USC medical
facility strikes a more ambiguous note than the tragic ending of the
Antigone. In fact, it brings to mind Aeschylus's ending in the *Oresteia*
where a wise Athena after affirming the public order persuades the
reluctant Furies, goddesses of the private and familial, to stay in
Athens where they will be cared for. That resolution, as Aeschylus
and Sophocles were both aware, was a tenuous reconciliation of
public and private. Ms. Bouvia's situation at the hospital has been
described as "an uneasy truce." Perhaps that is all that can be hoped
for in this imperfect world. Like the Furies, Ms. Bouvia has given
up her prerogatives; but, fortunately, there do seem to be some
medical staff at the Los Angeles/USC hospital who with Athena-
like wisdom perhaps have persuaded her to compromise and remain
with them. And with such a compromise where both parties pledge
to reconcile the competing claims of private right and public good,
might we not be able to discern behind the bonds of this "truce" a
real *koinōnia?*

I hope so. We began our consideration of the Elizabeth Bouvia case with the remark that underneath the claims and counterclaims lay some disturbing truths about ourselves as a civic people. For all her pluck in battling the full authority of the medical and legal profession, Elizabeth Bouvia seemed a lonely woman who felt abandoned by her own body, her lover, her society. The more unmanageable these relations became the more intractable she seemed to become, thus further alienating herself from the very community she desperately sought for support. For all the faults of this neoteric Antigone, much blame lies on the doorsteps of society also. No matter how righteous the cause, a people is simply mouthing words if it does not back up with caring deeds its claim that life is sacred. How a community treats its weakest and most vulnerable serves as an index of its moral fiber. That Elizabeth Bouvia and other handicapped persons feel so estranged from the community speaks not well of us. To object that she would not have felt so alienated if the courts had granted her wish only plunges us into a profound Sophoclean irony. We are more than happy to allow dissident Antigones to have their way, so long as their "way" is a taking leave of us in exile or death. Out of sight, out of care.[54] But that is not what the staff at the Los Angeles/USC hospital have done. Ms. Bouvia's fate may not be a happy one, but at least it is not Antigone's. A measure of joy, however small, might be found in that.

> Neither a life of anarchy
> Nor of despotism
> Should you praise.
> In all things it is the middle course that God grants dominion,
> But sometimes He ordains this path; at times another.
>   (Aeschylus, *Eumenides* 526–530)

This is the ancient wisdom. It might well be ours. But if we are to discern the right way—now this time, now the next—then we must cultivate a life of virtue that permits us to discern and emboldens us to act. It is to the consideration of public virtue that we now turn.

CHAPTER 3

Public Virtue: The Cyclopes Meet the Eastern Shore Watermen

❧

Non nobis solum nati sumus.—Cicero

When a man's in trouble, anybody hereabouts will risk his life
for him, don't matter what he thinks of him.—Waterman

B
easts or gods? How might Aristotle have categorized the one-
eyed Cyclopes of the *Odyssey*? Whatever their nature, these
"wondrous monsters" were certainly for the Greeks the paradigm of the unconnected, the un-citied, the un-political race.[1]
Despite their godlike size and stature, they lacked culture; namely,
agriculture, navigation and, above all, "deliberative assemblies"
(*agorai boulephoroi*) (*Odyssey* 9.112). In the illustrious choral ode of the
Antigone, Sophocles offers a striking and probably conscious contrast
to these "awe-ful" creatures; it is the "wondrously strange mortals"
who "navigate the perilous seas . . . plow the difficult earth . . . and
build themselves cities."[2] It is one of these mortals, the wily
Odysseus, who tricks and vanquishes the great Cyclops Polyphemus.
Unable to match the Cyclops's strength, the "ever resourceful"
Odysseus manages, along with his comrades, to gouge out the crea-
ture's eye and escape his cave under the bellies of sheep and a ram.
While Polyphemus had received a prophetic warning about this
character Odysseus, the Cyclops in his hubris had expected someone
at least as large and magnificent as himself. Instead he is bested, as
he cries out at the end of the episode, by a weak "nobody."

The familiar image of the lawless Cyclopes might be an appropriate place to begin a chapter on public virtue. Civilization is born out of the Cyclopes' cave; the dispositions needed for the transition from autonomy to community shine forth in the reverse image of Polyphemus's inhospitable character. A discussion of public virtue and vice cannot proceed without models, and what makes the Cyclopes such an instructive image is not that they represent public vice—bad civic habits develop *within* the context of community—but rather that their character is so apolitical. Here perhaps is the closest Greek equivalent to a Hobbesian natural state where creatures show no inclination to speak about what is good and bad, about what is just and unjust. A discussion of the struggle between Polyphemus and Odysseus's men might well capture the specific virtue that characterizes the transition from a pre-political to a political existence.

If public virtues are those habitual ways of acting that foster the common good, the Cyclopes are notably without them. These are solitary creatures, likened by Homer to isolated trees standing alone on a lofty mountain peak.[3] They do not care for or associate with each other, preferring instead to live apart without any higher political order (*themis*). They do lay down the law (*themisteuei*) for their wives and children, but it is not accidental, I imagine, that Polyphemus, the most illustrious of them (*poly-phemus*), is presented by Homer as unwed and childless.[4] He is a truly autonomous character.

It is almost as though the gods had been too generous to these giants. Their island is almost Edenlike; they need not toil nor spin. Without nature's harshness, they have not experienced the need for self-restraint, that discipline and disposition we mortals find indispensable for a communal existence. Like the dinosaurs, their development is one-dimensional: sheer physical size and strength at the expense of thought and joint endeavors. That thoughtless isolation was, of course, Polyphemus's undoing. Unlike the physically weaker, "bread-eating" race of mortals, who must rely on one another to survive, these people-eating monsters are locked into their own appetites. Polyphemus impiously mocks "Zeus-Xenios," the "Protector of Guests," by announcing to Odysseus that he will eat him last, his "hospitality gift" for the good wine Odysseus brought. That act places him in direct opposition to the moral core of the *Odyssey* and the ultimate test of a community's character— care for the stranger.⁵

Now the story of Odysseus's encounter with the Cyclopes is itself rather strange. Western civilization has traveled a long way from Homer's Ithaca. But beneath the layered vestiges of our historical transformations, we can yet recognize ourselves in Homer's text as the "bread-eating" two-eyed mortals who, as beings who know both good and evil, look to past and future and care for self and other. It is still the human condition to plow the earth, sail the seas, and attend long-winded *agorai boulephoroi* (public assemblies)! As a case in point, permit me to introduce the Tilghman Island watermen.

Near where I live and teach lies an island where generations of watermen have sought their livelihood in the depths of the Chesapeake Bay and its tributaries. Perhaps a brief look at this island community, not so unlike Odysseus's beloved Ithaca, might help us forge some connecting links between Homeric virtues and our own habits of the heart.

Like many traditional American communities, these Tilghman Islanders are rugged, fiercely independent, highly competitive, yet bonded deeply with each other and the sea. Unlike the Cyclopes, it is very much a human community; that is to say, its virtues and its vices are forged out of the community's history and tradition. (Their storytelling could enthrall even a Homer!) Its people can display a wariness, even hostility, toward the outsider and a fierce and sometimes shortsighted protectiveness of their harvesting of the Chesapeake Bay's resources. The petty jealousies and quarrels that are part and parcel of closely knit communities can be found here also. And yet a cooperative spirit runs as surely and deeply among them as the channels that run by their island. Their homespun wisdom is as simple and clever as their crab traps. Their quick wit solders their affection for one another and serves to deflate even the hint of pretentiousness. While they are understandably guarded toward strangers, their displays of hospitality are legendary on the Eastern Shore of Maryland. My wife had occasion once to extend a simple favor to one of the islanders and, in return, we received what

Homer called "hospitality gifts," almost as lavish and certainly as unstintingly proffered as any received by Odysseus.

My point in introducing the contrast between these islanders and the Cyclopes is nothing very dramatic. I do not wish to romanticize the watermen, for in some sense it is their very ordinariness that is important here. There are perhaps a number of communities like them, and certainly there are many little communities that flourish anonymously within the larger more impersonal urban and rural population centers. However, those latter communities are more difficult to see and analyze; the advantage of an island community, like a Platonic myth, is that its very isolation allows the character of a people to reveal itself unmixed with all the other divergent landscapes that make up our political geography. So, let us explore a bit the character of these Tilghman Islanders.[6]

The island itself is small. Cut off from the mainland by a 150-foot channel—Knapps Narrows—it stretches only three and a half miles to its southernmost extension at Walnut Point. Its width barely reaches a mile. Still, it serves as port and home for about fifteen hundred people, mostly watermen and their families who harvest the bay's once rich resources of crabs, clams, and oysters. It may not look like Ithaca, but I suspect Odysseus would feel more at home here than in most other places today!

A visitor to Tilghman will be accorded a hospitable but somewhat guarded reception. Should the guest, however, have a host on the island (in Homeric Greek *Xenos* can mean both "guest" and "host") the reception is much more open and cordial. And what becomes apparent to the guest who partakes in the rounds of their lives on the water, at their feasts, at funerals and at weddings, is that here is an almost self-sufficient community that shares common purposes. Writing about a similar community in Port Royal, Kentucky, Wendell Berry characterized it as "successful and effective" because "it did what a good community does. It supported itself, amused itself, consoled itself, and passed its knowledge on to the young."[7] That could be said of the Tilghman Island watermen; and unfortunately, like the farmers in Port Royal, their way of life seems to be rapidly disappearing. But that is another story; my purpose here is to capture the dispositions that distinguish the character of the watermen from the Cyclopes. To do that, we might look at them at work on the water, certainly their most distinguishing and characteristic activity, and in a locale, Homer is careful to note, where the Cyclopes never dared to venture.[8]

As viewed through the eyes of a guest, life on the water seems incredibly arduous: up at 4:00 A.M., long hours in the summer heat or bone-chilling autumnal winds, uncertain conditions in the seas and in the market, increasing competition for depleting stocks of oysters, clams, and crabs. Perhaps it is these very hardships, in contrast to the lush Cyclopean land, that account for the cooperative spirit among these watermen. While they have to face an increasing number of external government regulations—grumbling against them has been raised by the islanders to a high art—for the most part they regulate themselves. An unwritten, informal, yet quite complex code regulates their movements and insures a fair distribution of the seas' resources.[9] Without such a code one could easily imagine daily—even hourly—squabbles over who goes where and gets what. Hostilities that erupt usually do so when different communities collide over the use of the same area of the Bay. Internal disputes, of course, also occur, though they seem much less frequent than in other occupations and, again, informal codes spell out how they are resolved. One of the obvious functions of such codes is to create an efficient and trouble-free harvesting of the sea; but it would be a mistake, I think, to interpret such a code only in economic terms. The code does not create the community; rather, it is only out of an already developed communal life that such a code can develop. The code of the water ensures that justice is served, but the communal arrangements require even more. If a boat is in distress, help comes immediately and without regard to the day's lost catch. If one of their members is down on his luck, others rally to his assistance, providing machinery, even a boat if necessary, to help a neighbor get back on his feet.

This kind of communal life cannot help but create a communal character. The concord displayed on the seas and back at home would not be possible without considerable self-restraint. Self-disciplined these people certainly are (the harsh realities of their livelihood weed out the slacker); but even more remarkable is their self-restraint. Few are tempted to take at the expense of another. Like Odysseus's men they have learned the efficacy of cooperation and restraint of their more immediate impulses. But such restraint is not a calculation aimed at self-interested ends; rather it is a virtue that emerges from the requirements of living together. Self-restraint is, as the Greeks thought, not the highest but certainly the first of those dispositions that create a communal life. Let us look at that virtue a bit more closely.

In *The Philosopher in the City*, Hadley Arkes nicely captures the political force of self-restraint:

> It has traditionally been thought that a man who can restrain himself out of respect for some other interest than his own, someone who shows in the ordinary course of his life a sense of obligation to family, friends or community is a far better man, a far more human and civilized being than one who respects no law beyond his own self-interest.[10]

So crucial is this disposition for a polity that Arkes says we measure the goodness of communities more by "the conditions of civility" than "the supply of amenities."[11] That nicely captures the distinction between the Achaeans and the Cyclopean way of life, but there is little doubt that in today's world exhortations to restraint are more likely to be met with skepticism, if not outright disdain.

Any restraints upon the self, even when they are self-imposed, inevitably create the fear in a liberal society that individuality will be sacrificed in the name of a higher public good. That is a legitimate concern, particularly since, in the United States, the public good contains as one of its most fundamental purposes the fostering of its citizens' liberty. We need, therefore, to look more closely at what exactly gets sacrificed in self-restraint.

Self-restraint is not self-immolation. Here, again, the Cyclopes are instructive. They are creatures of immediate desires. Polyphemus's only concession to restraint seems to have been in not eating all of Odysseus's men at once but only two at a time. Not without reason does Homer characterize these creatures as not knowing right from wrong. Only in the experience of the difference between what I want and what is good, between desire and obligation, can the moral life and, perforce, the communal life be born. Polyphemus need only consult his desires to determine what to do; mortals like Odysseus must employ reason—*logos*—to decipher what ought to be done. In that distance between immediate desire and reflection lies the difference, as Aristotle put it, between beasts and ourselves. Because they are creatures of their desires, the Cyclopes' growth has been all one-dimensional—sheer size and physical stature. Mortals who "have learned speech and wispy thought and political virtue (*astunomous orgas*)"[12]—as Sophocles puts it—must check their passions and let those higher but less immediate "desires" seek fulfillment.

What is sacrificed in self-restraint, then, is not the self but, rather, those unchecked appetites, so powerful because they are so immediate, that destroy the only life that is good for mortals, the life in a community. I wonder if one of the reasons Odysseus's wine offering to Polyphemus tasted so good was due to the Cyclopes' unwillingness to spend the time to make good, aged wine! Certainly a cooked meal involves the sacrifice of the immediate pangs of appetite. If restraint cannot be shown here, how much more difficult it would be when it comes to the enjoyment of community life. Just as the restraining of one's sexual desires allows for the possibility that spousal and parental relationships will flourish, so the restraint of one's individual interests allows for the possibility of civic relationships to blossom.

Even if we grant that self-restraint is necessary for a commodious communal life, it does not follow that self-interest is thereby transcended. If our best interest as humans is preserved by restraining our most immediate drives for the sake of less immediate but more fulfilling goals, then it hardly seems necessary to speak of the sacrifice of self-interest in the name of a higher public good. To return to the example of the Tilghman Islanders, might it not be claimed that it is in each waterman's long-term interest to develop the cooperative arrangement by which he earns his living? Perhaps there is no real qualitative difference between these watermen and the Cyclopes; rather, only a more sophisticated calculation of what works to advance an individual's survival distinguishes the former from the latter.

The ethical assumption that all our moral acts are nothing more than expressions of self-interest has managed, at least in the Western tradition, to capture a small but tenacious following. That view is increasingly discredited today, and in chapter 2 I attempted to demonstrate how a philosophy of self-interest does little justice to the richness of our communal life. Indeed, to believe that every moral act is but an instrument of my own interest utterly violates the very meaning of a shared relationship. In this chapter, however, I want to look at the issue from a more practical, more political vantage point. If we pay close attention to the way Americans speak and justify their own acts, particularly their generous deeds, you cannot help but notice, as Alexis de Tocqueville did, their reluctance to characterize their services to their neighbors in altruistic or purely selfless terms. "He'd a done the same for me" is a justification that could come as easily from the lips of our Tilghman Islander as it did from Tocqueville's nineteenth-century farmer. His commentary on the American tendency to substitute the language of self-interest for the older traditional discourse of self-sacrifice contains some of Tocqueville's most profound and perplexing thoughts on the American character. In those pages, Tocqueville presents us with the claim (in perhaps its most sophisticated and reflective form) that the lofty tradition of public virtue must give way to the more modern pedestrian behavioral norm of "self-interest rightly understood."[13] We need to look carefully at that argument.

To begin, let us return to that self-effacing retort, "He'd a done the same for me," and note how deceptive such a simple phrase can be. Instead of seeing it as a straightforward appeal to self-interest as some theorists might do, Tocqueville noted the ambiguity, even the inconsistency, in how the Americans justified their generous deeds in terms of "private interest" despite the "disinterested and spontaneous impulses" from which such deeds sprang (p. 130). By their inattention to the discrepancy between the motivation and the justification of their acts, Tocqueville believed the "Americans fail to do themselves justice" and were "more anxious to do honor to their philosophy than to themselves" (pp. 130–131).

Now, what is at stake here is much more than a mere linguistic discrepancy or a false humility on the part of early nineteenth-century Americans. Tocqueville's analysis penetrates more deeply into the heart of the American experience. He believed that the democratic revolution, with its creation of universal equality, was actually effacing the noble impulses to be virtuous. The pragmatic philosophy of the Americans was not some abstract theoretical overlay but actually expressed an understanding of an emergent egalitarian world. People would no longer act on behalf of their fellow citizens because it was "noble to make such sacrifices" but because it was in their interest to do so. In a democratic revolution equality eliminates *noblesse oblige*. What is expected of one must be expected of all. Tocqueville thought it the prudent thing, then, to make modest demands upon the citizens, lest the appeal to heroic virtue fall on deaf ears and in its stead the more immediate and urgent cry of egoism stifle any moral sensibility.

The philosophy of self-interest rightly understood is then, for Tocqueville, a political compromise, a middle way between the lofty but unattainable practice of noble virtue and the base but relentless drive of selfish interests. Succinctly put, the principle of self-interest rightly understood, while directing a person to follow his or her self-interest, demonstrates that it is in each person's interest to be virtuous. It is, or so Tocqueville thought, a philosophy particularly adapted to the democratic spirit of the times—and absolutely necessary if the democratic revolution was not to degenerate into a self-destructive egoism. While such a principle is "not a lofty one," it is "clear and sure" and, most importantly, "lies within the reach of all capacities . . . by its admirable conformity to human weaknesses" (p. 131). While it "produces no great acts of self-sacrifice," it "suggests small daily acts of self-denial," and while it doesn't "make a man virtuous," it produces habits of "regularity, temperance, moderation, foresight, self-command" (p. 131). Tocqueville foresaw a day when "personal interest will become more than ever the principal if not the sole spring of men's actions" (p. 132). Self-interest rightly understood would at least check "the pitch of stupid excesses" our selfishness leads to. Rather than correct our selfishness with virtue, a strategy more conducive to aristocratic times, Tocqueville thought that, in a democratic polity, interest is better checked by interest, passion by passion. Here, then, was the new task of a democratic *paideia*, educating the masses "to sacrifice something of their well-being to the prosperity of their fellow creatures" (p. 132).

In these pages of *Democracy in America*, Tocqueville touches upon one of the oldest and most intractable issues in public philosophy: public character. How does one develop in citizens a disposition to act on behalf of the public good? To wrestle with that question plunges one further into the very depths of moral and public philosophy: the question of evil in a society and how best to respond to it. No wonder Tocqueville was tempted to excuse himself from the debate because of "the extreme difficulty of the subject" (p. 130). Fortunately, he had too much intellectual integrity to finesse the topic and so we can still today benefit by his wisdom—even if we will not completely agree with him. A word of caution may well be in order here, however. No less than Tocqueville, we ought to be aware of the subject's difficulty; what follows should be seen as more probative than definitive.

Given that cautionary note, what can be said about this issue of public character? First of all, some thinkers, both ancient and modern, conservative and liberal, have despaired of ever developing dispositions for the public good in the mass of citizens and, instead, have pinned their hopes on the formation of a "few good [and invariably] men." This is hardly the place for a long digression on elites. Suffice it to say that, while elites, like the poor, will (probably) always be with us, they create more problems for public character than they solve. Even if we granted that a virtuous elite (that is, an elite that truly acted for the common good) could be established, it still leaves unanswered the question of the relationship of the elite to the masses. Even to expect (blind?) obedience is to raise the troubling query of how to instill that and why the masses would be receptive to such an arrangement. Furthermore, there seems to be a fundamental difference between the natural and unplanned evolution of an elite (of whatever sort) and the intentional creation and management of one in politics. Even the Greek theorists, often the staunchest defenders of the rule of the best, admitted that aristocracy inevitably degenerated into oligarchy.

Tocqueville was a more courageous and ultimately, I think, a more realistic thinker. He was willing to tackle the issue of public character in a democracy, and he felt he could do it because he had seen in America overwhelming evidence that a character disposed toward the public good was already developing. More modest than the old order's lofty ideals, it nonetheless was effective in holding a community together—effective, as he said, "because it so "admirably conformed to human weaknesses" (p. 131). That is the key to understanding Tocqueville's view of politics. His view of the human condition was neither overly optimistic nor unduly pessimistic. Like Madison before him, he saw that the ordinary run of humanity was neither angelic nor beastly. It was perfectly appropriate then, he felt, to pay attention to the legal and institutional supports for being good. For most of us most of the time the moral life is a rather mundane struggle, and in that struggle we need all the help we can get. If that means we need to see that good will be rewarded and evil punished, then so be it. After all, even Socrates, that most noble defender of virtue itself, took pains to show Crito the evil consequences that follow an evil act.[14] In his exasperation with his fellow French citizens who talked in terms of lofty virtue while at the same time acting utterly selfishly, Tocqueville exclaimed: "Will nobody undertake to make them understand how what is right may be useful?" (p. 132). What Tocqueville is pointing out here, namely the responsibility we have to make the public good attractive and public evil repulsive, is a truth often neglected by those liberals who rant against any government involvement in the sphere of morality and those conservatives who rail against government regulations in the marketplace. Government intrusion can be baneful, but what good community would not be concerned about sexual license and rampant greed?

I had a married colleague who once confided to me that he no longer was tempted to run around, not because of any moral inhibition but because it was, as he put it, "too much of a hassle." One could hardly applaud his virtue, but for the sake of his wife and future paramours, we might be grateful for the impediments. By the same token, when a recent British newspaper account revealed that 11 percent of the men and 3 percent of the women polled would commit murder to become millionaires if assured they would not be caught, we might be chagrined by the results yet relieved that the possibility of being caught forestalls so many homicides. Would it not be masochistic or, worse, the essence of conceit to wish to live in a community where evil is unrestrained by laws and mores just so the good can prove their virtue? What more cogent reason could be advanced for tax reform than the current system's discouragement through inequities and loopholes of any sense of public-mindedness? We could be cynical about such slogans as "good ethics is good business," but would we prefer a community where good ethics is bad business? There is always the danger, of course, that by making goodness "pay off" we promote the misconception that one should be good *because* it pays. But, again, surely that danger is preferable to a situation where goodness and utility are not confused because being good is never a profitable thing.

Tocqueville's analysis presents us with a powerful reminder of our public responsibility to see that what Cicero called the *bonum honestum* (the morally good) and the *bonum utile* (the usefully good) are conjoined as much as possible. The question remains, however, whether or not his rejection of a political virtue in favor of self-interest rightly understood actually does justice to American practice. Let us return to our Tilghman Islander in the hope of receiving some enlightenment on that point.

We have already attended to the ambiguity Tocqueville might see in an expression such as "He'd a done the same for me." We need to explore that ambiguity even further. The fact that a neighbor would reciprocate a favor does not necessarily mean that the initial deed was done *because* the favor could be returned. The Tilghman waterman would have to be a rather calculating character for the doctrine of self-interest rightly understood to apply here. This means he would have to go to the assistance of another waterman in trouble and lose valuable time because he calculates that he might be similarly situated some day. While that is certainly a possible, though I think an overly abstract, reading of the situation, it is more likely that the expression, so effortless on the part of the waterman, is less a rationale and more a description of simply what is. "He'd a done the same for me" simply reports on what it means to live in this community where each does for the other. Instead of a self-interested calculation, the characteristic expression of the Tilghman Islanders reports an expectation and a responsibility. This is what it means to live in a community—recall (in chapter 2) the Athenian shrines to the *Charites*, the goddesses of dispensing and receiving favors. The islanders expect favors to be returned because it is the nature of a good community to do so. "If we don't help each other from time to time, who will?" That self-deflating but hardly self-interested remark came from a waterman who was trying to explain why he and his "fellow drudgers" would spend extra hours on the water dredging clams for a sick waterman back on the island.[15]

That example, common among these men, stands in sharp contrast to the hotshot young junk bond dealers of the 1980s who cared little for the suffering imposed on workers laid off as a result of the corporate take-overs. When not hedged in by strong, communal ties, capitalism can clearly wreak havoc with peoples' lives. The watermen, fierce competitors that they are, seem to know this. "Two things are certain," Mike Blackestone writes: "Watermen are always in competition with each other for products and looking out for each other's welfare at the same time."[16] With the same vigilance that they must use to watch the winds and the seas, with that same care they look out for one another. Whether or not one watches out for one's fellow neighbor depends less, then, on how self-interested or altruistic one is and much more on how close the common ties are that bind us.

The standard modern way of framing the character issue—self-interest versus altruism—is too abstract and therefore terribly misguided. The emphasis is on the individual: shall I act in my own interest or leave it aside and act on behalf of others? The more fundamental and realistic question is: What are the demands of living together? As I pointed out in chapter 2, we are conceived, nurtured, born, raised, and buried within a community. Our existence is always already communal and our moral and political obligations spring from this fundamental reality. Certainly we are capable of acting selfishly or, for that matter, altruistically; but our moral bearings come from the fact that we are beings who dwell in a community.

The concept of self-interest rightly understood, insofar as it cuts between pure self-interest and altruism, is itself framed by individualism. Tocqueville readily admits that, because he sees the American experience as so decidedly individualistic. It may be that, as he argues, Americans do not do themselves justice when it comes to their selfless deeds; it may also be true that Tocqueville himself does not do them justice either. We get a glimpse of that when we turn to what he rightly identifies as the corrective to self-interest: free institutions.

When they take part in public affairs, Americans, Tocqueville believed, are "drawn from the circle of their own interests and snatched . . . from self-observation" (p. 109). In the peculiarly American penchant (some might say "obsession") for associations— civil and social—can be found the remedy for individualism. But even here he identifies the motivation for "acting in concert" as their "interest to forget themselves" (p. 110). But if acting on behalf of the public involves, as Tocqueville claims, "a long succession of little services rendered and obscure good deeds, a constant habit of kindness, and an established reputation for *disinterestedness*" (emphasis mine, p. 111), then I think that disinterest entails a level of virtue and public-mindedness distinctly above self-interest, even when "rightly understood." Hannah Arendt, herself a great admirer of Tocqueville, nonetheless argued that "to recognize and embrace the common good requires not enlightened self-interest but impartiality," like the impartiality required of jurors who must act out of something "outside themselves which makes them common."[17]

I am not sure why Tocqueville, who otherwise was such a perceptive commentator on the American scene, failed to recognize the phenomenon of impartiality as distinct from interest. I suspect that, in part, it had to do with his identification of a virtue ethic with the old aristocratic order; the alternative, new, democratic order expressed a radically different ethos of individualism. So, for him, one either did something because it was the noble thing to do or because it involved self-interest (even when rightly understood). Our Tilghman Islanders point, however, to a third possibility. They would hardly characterize even their most selfless deeds as "noble," but neither would they be comfortable, I suspect, with the categories of calculated self-interest. It is, rather, the virtuous disposition to act for others that is cradled in their homes, nurtured in their churches, and continually practiced on the water. It is this virtuous character that distinguishes them from the Cyclopes and reveals them as a people more civilized than some of the more sophisticated "communities" whose members care not one whit about each other.

This rather prolonged critique of self-interest has also taken us a good way down the road from self-restraint. We have now arrived at the very soul of public virtue: that is, the disposition that unites the members of a public community. As necessary as self-restraint is for the formation of a community, it is hardly sufficient to provide the glue that keeps members together. It is, I believe, vitally important that we get this right; for just as we can underestimate the public spirit with such categories as self-interest rightly understood, so we can expect too much of civic virtue. It would be possible to sentimentalize the people of Tilghman, imagining an intimacy and devotedness that is not there. But even more dangerous for our purposes would be to model the public bonds of citizenship on the intimacy of lovers or on the natural affinities of families. Whatever hopes we may have for it, the civic community is not first and foremost a "beloved community." To assume it is or should be is an invitation to despair or tyranny. Impetuous youth (though not all the young are impetuous nor all the impetuous ones young) often grow impatient with the contentious ways of public life and despair of it ever achieving their lofty communal goals. Their retreat into the private and intimate worlds of friends and loved ones leaves the public bereft of their presence and puts a perhaps insupportable burden on private relationships. Such despair, as damaging as it is to the civic community, is nothing compared to the tyrannizing efforts of those who would transform the public by whatever means into their cherished but unrealistic dreams. If there is to be an alternative to the Jacobins' "Be my brother or die," it must lie in a spirit that is neither meanly self-serving nor overly romantic.

It is Aristotle, that philosopher of the middle way, who, I think, most clearly identifies that virtue. In a little gem of a chapter in the *Nichomachean Ethics* (chapter 6 of book 9), he discusses the type of friendship (*philia*) peculiar to the "citizens of a *polis*." He calls it "*homonoia*," literally "like-mindedness," and it often is translated in English by "concord," that is, "like-heartedness." When the hearts and minds of citizens are in unanimity, then civic harmony is possible. This virtue is neither self-serving nor is it as intimate as some friendships. Such amity concerns "practical ends" as when citizens agree about their purposes and carry them out. It concerns, Aristotle declares, both "the right and the useful" and thereby captures what Tocqueville was seeking for but inadequately expressed with the doctrine of self-interest rightly understood. It also expresses well, I think, the public-mindedness and cooperative spirit of the Tilghman Islanders.

The opposite of *homonoia* is *stasiōtikos*, discord and factionalism. That contentious spirit is caused, Aristotle argues, when citizens of bad character want more than their just share and shirk their obligations of "work and public service." *Homonoia*, however, the spirit of public amity, is created when citizens act in concert. It does not make them lovers nor brothers and sisters; rather, it makes them friendly, trustworthy, dependable, whatever makes citizens good citizens.[18] In *homonoia* and *stasiōtikos* we have the specific virtue and vice that foster or diminish the reciprocity of communal life (*koinōnia*). One can find it among the Tilghman Islanders as well as Tocqueville's farmers. One can find it less easily, perhaps, in small, well-defined communities in our cities and towns. And, unfortunately, we can readily find its opposite, contentiousness, in those places rural and urban, in the ghettos and on Wall Street, where the hearts and minds of citizens seek only to secure their own private advantage.

If public virtue begins in self-restraint and if it abides in unanimity of minds and hearts, then in what does it find its end or fulfillment? What is the final test and ultimate expression of public virtue? We began with Odysseus emerging from the Cyclopes' cave, traced virtue through the nineteenth-century farmer and twentieth-century waterman. Now to bring this journey to an end, we need to visit the villagers in the small town of Le Chambon-sur-Lignon in southern France. For it is there we will uncover what C. S. Lewis called "the *experimentum crucis*" of virtue. Here we find the crucible where not only is self-interest burned out but even *homonoia* is refined into the higher order of charity. In the willingness of the citizens of Le Chambon to risk all for the sake of the stranger, we have the ultimate expression of sacrifice for the sake of a transcendent, communal good.

I have postponed until now consideration of the heroic community not because such a community is not a persuasive refutation of self-interest—it is, indeed—but because if we had too quickly jumped to the crossroads experience we might create again the very dichotomy Tocqueville sought to avoid: heroism or selfishness. The via media had to be first identified and accurately described, and only then could we more safely turn to the transformation of *homonoia* into *caritas*. Radical conversion is certainly possible, but communities are less likely than individuals to be the subject of radical transformation. That can be a bane as well as a boon, but it demonstrates how important it is that a community be gradually built up by those modest deeds Tocqueville praised before it can respond well to the test by fire. Such a test may well separate the sheep from the goats; but, as I have already mentioned, citizens ought not seek it out lest we discover the goat in us all. An individual like Socrates may well shine forth against the dark background of a corrupt polity; but communities, if they are to be beacons in a dark world, must first cultivate good laws, good institutions, good character. And that is exactly what happened in the little town of Le Chambon.

The story of the people of Le Chambon and their pastor, Andre Trocmé, and how they successfully harbored Jewish refugees during the course of World War II has been beautifully told in literature (*Lest Innocent Blood Be Shed* by Philip Hallie) and in film (*Weapons of the Spirit*). I will not attempt to retell that story here; rather I would let the remarkable spirit of the Chambonnais serve as an illumination for some thoughts on what makes a community heroic.

We might, first off, remark on the self-effacing way these villagers characterized efforts that others would describe as morally laudatory. Every time a welcoming door was opened to Jewish refugees, each member of this Protestant community knew well his or her fate could be sealed with that act. But, characteristically, when the villagers were asked about the risk, the reply would be: "Well, where else could they go? I had to take them in."[19] Of course, there were other alternatives; they could have turned the fleeing Jews over to the authorities. What they were expressing was a moral and religious necessity. Their character and faith left them no alternative. They knew full well the fate of these Jewish refugees if they didn't take them in and they responded according to the dictates of their conscience. It would ring falsely to say they risked their lives out of self-interest. Of them, Mary Midgley's words seem particularly apropos:

> It is indeed possible to describe their behavior by saying that they did what they really wanted and many moralists have used this language. But there is something slightly wild and paradoxical about this way of talking when in a perfectly obvious sense these people did what they were terrified to do, and did it because they thought they ought to.[20]

Unlike the thirty-eight people in the now infamous Kitty Genovese slaying who heard her anguished screams and pleas for help and did nothing out of fear of getting involved, here an entire village daily risked their lives and property because of the Christian scripture's injunction to welcome the stranger.[21]

Indeed, what possible self-interest might the Chambonnais have had? Religious gains? Not likely. The only reported conversion during the entire period was a villager to Judaism.[22] Personal salvation? Hardly. It is clear from all the extensive interviews that the villagers acted out of their love for God and neighbor rather than out of what George Eliot called "egoism turned heavenward." While heaven was something believed in and hoped for, it is clear that they did not rescue Jews in order to merit memberships in the community of saints.[23] They were, after all, devout descendants of Huguenots! No, what was formed in Le Chambon was one of those "communities of character," which, in Michael Walzer's words, represent "historically stable, ongoing associations of men and women with some special commitment to one another and some special sense of their common life."[24] In this case, their special commitment was to their religious faith, which led them to welcome the stranger at considerable personal risk.

How ironic, and yet how fitting, that the ultimate test of a community's character is not how it takes care of its own but its willingness to take in the alien, the stranger. If there is a theme more fertile, more mysterious in our aesthetic, philosophical, and religious tradition than that of the stranger, I am not aware of it. It is an inexhaustible source of moral reflection. Here, I can only hint at a few points that shed light on the importance of the stranger for a community of character.

The stranger is, first of all, a sign of contradiction.[25] Threatening and yet vulnerable, the stranger is a source of terror and fascination, an image of both the demonic and the divine. The hostile stranger can disrupt, even destroy a community. Homer recounts that Odysseus, that "sacker of cities," utterly destroyed Ismoros, the first city he "visited" after the destruction of Troy. But even the more innocent stranger can be a source of danger. The people of Le Chambon were well aware of what peril they took upon themselves by welcoming Jewish refugees. Even in his more friendly arrival among the Phaiacians, the stranger-guest Odysseus brought trouble in his wake. When they graciously conveyed him back to Ithaca, Poseidon destroyed their glorious ship as punishment. We cannot help but sympathize with King Alcinoos when he ruefully proclaims to the Phaiacians: "Give no more convoy to strangers who shall come to our city."[26] Prudence would argue caution in the presence of some strangers.

Cautious, even devilishly deceptive, the people of Le Chambon could be, especially to the Vichy authorities. When asked to provide a list of Jewish names to the authorities, Pastor Trocmé would always reply he didn't know the names of any Jews in his town. He, in fact, didn't, because the refugees were cautioned, for safety's sake, not to reveal their real names to anyone. Yet when it came to welcoming and harboring the strangers who arrived at their back doors, the Chambonnais threw caution to the winds. They were, for the most part, poor villagers, yet they shared whatever they had with their guests whom they named simply and aptly *les enfants de Dieu* (God's children). A strikingly similar gesture of hospitality is recorded by Homer when he has the simple swineherd Eumaios say to Odysseus, "Stranger-guests . . . are sent to us by the gods."[27]

What accounts for such lavishness in the face of the potential danger the stranger brings? Why is the stranger seen as the epiphany of the divine? Why would the test of a people's piety be how gracious their welcoming of the stranger could be?

It would be facile and cynical to say that such hospitality rites were simply the necessary underwriting of commerce. Undoubtedly, trade could hardly flourish if every stranger-guest either murdered or was murdered by his host. Polyphemus cared nothing for trade and so could scoff at Odysseus's appeal to observe the rites of hospitality. But whatever the beneficial consequences for commerce, the grounds for the care of the stranger lie much deeper. An economic interpretation is a classic case of putting the cart laden with goods before the horse that drives it. What drove Odysseus was not trade but his desire to return to his beloved Ithaca; the stranger-guests at Le Chambon brought with them no goods but their humanity. It is to that humanity, naked and vulnerable, that the people of Chambon and the hospitable swineherd responded. It is in the fearful, defenseless look of the stranger that we see ourselves. We welcome the stranger for we recognize him or her as ourself. The lonely, forsaken stranger represents the human condition at its worst, without the succor of communal love. To rescue and harbor the stranger is not just to save his or her life, it is also to save the human being from its most wretched condition, the condition of being without a city (*a-polis*), without a nurturing community.

In chapter 2 I attempted a philosophical critique of the autonomous individual; here we have a more powerful existential refutation. In his or her vulnerability lies the truth about myself: I am not autonomous. Each of us must rely, as certain Southern ladies say, upon the kindness of strangers. To be the recipient of that favor is to be a guest. In the face of the stranger, then, lies the truth of community: we need each other. Sharing—*koinōnein*—is at the root of the human condition. Those who share well, with excellence, as the people of Le Chambon did, are the truly virtuous.

Such virtue does not come easy; it demands courage, loyalty, and ultimately a willingness to risk all for the sake of the other. It is no wonder that such heroic public virtue most often wells up from religious piety. In the *Odyssey*, Athena is disguised in the dress of a miserable old hag; in the Christian scriptures, Christ is present in the poor, the lowly, the sick, and the imprisoned. The divine is totally other and yet within us; no wonder then that the mysterious stranger would signify the presence of God among us.

While it may be that the kind of heroism the people of Le Chambon demonstrated in World War II is only understood in the bedrock of their faith, the issue of the stranger is one that must be faced by any political community, sacred or secular. Strangers without a political community are stateless people, and stateless-ness, as Michael Walzer notes, "is a condition of infinite danger."[28] If the communal sharing of a community expresses the deepest meaning of the human condition, then those human beings deprived of such membership because they are refugees, resident aliens, guest workers, require a community's special attention. The problems such strangers create are not easily resolved, but I suggest that the measure by which we judge our response to political refugees in this country might well be the spirit in which the Chambonnais welcomed the Jews in Nazi controlled France.

The course of life in most of our communities lies between the inhospitable caves of the Cyclopes and the heroic welcome of the people of Le Chambon. Like the Tilghman Islanders we sense that public virtue is not easily won but it is not impossible either. And we can take some small comfort in knowing that, in acting kindly toward others, most likely our neighbors "would a done the same for us."

CHAPTER 4

Public Speech: The Barbarian in the Brooks Brothers Suit

◯◯

Reverse Images

An image: El Salvador, 1980. A country tattered by violence; the fabric of its society rent with a seemingly endless cycle of vengeance; a *polis* where the lineaments of justice were no longer discernible. In a dispatch to the *Washington Post*, dated June 13, Christopher Dickey, a reporter who had been chronicling what he termed "the gradual destruction of Salvadoran society," had this to say: "Each side talks of justice: the revolutionary or peoples' justice of the left assassinates anyone suspected of being an informer; . . . the justice of the right . . . ends with the murder of anyone who might concede an inch of power or influence to the left. In the end, there is little or no justice."[1]

Dickey's depiction of a "climate of vengeance" in which the "bonds of human relationships" have been broken is hardly novel.[2] Indeed, we already have had occasion, in chapter 2, to locate the *locus classicus* of such a tale: Aeschylus's trilogy, the *Oresteia*. There too, in Argos, "where unto every doer is done," the "avenging gore" spills out over the land, and a father who sacrifices his daughter is, in turn, slain by his wife who subsequently is brutally dispatched by her son.[3] Both images—not timeless but certainly perennial—portray a violated public world where vengeance is mistaken for justice and furtive deceit masquerades as public discourse. In these lands barbarity has vanquished civility.

It is not my purpose, here, to retell that tragic story but rather to reverse those images, as in a camera obscura, so that they might reflect on something quite the opposite—the much more mundane and familiar tradition of civil discourse. In the spirit of G. K. Chesterton, who urged thinkers to look at the familiar until it became strange, I would like to view our civil speech, the *civilis conversatio* (to borrow Aquinas's alien tongue), in much the same way that Aeschylus used the barbarity of Argos to remind his fellow Athenians that the honey-lipped persuasion they took so much for granted was the wonderfully strange and fragile gift of a beneficent goddess. I do this because Chesterton's counsel was no mere theoretical trope but, rather, a practical mandate. History has taught us that the civilizing gift of a free and public discourse, once taken for granted, can easily be lost. Even more ominously, that forfeiture need not be effected, as Tocqueville reminded us, by barbarians outside the city walls, but may result from an inner barbarism that can lead the citizens to, quite willingly, "loosen their hold" on the bonds that join them together.[4]

The Strangeness of Mortals

How can something so familiar, so "perfectly natural," as the discourse that permeates our public lives—how can that phenomenon be viewed as strange? Only, perhaps, if we think back on a more fundamental strangeness, that of humanity itself. "Much there is that is strange but nothing so strange as man" (*Antigone* 332).[5] With those words, Sophocles opens his famous ode on man in the *Antigone*. What is so strange, so terrifying, and so filled with wonder is that these beings exist at all—these strange beings whose wit and power have enabled them to master the creatures of the earth and sea and yet who are so strangely fragile that they cannot flee, much less master, the one thing they most want to avoid—their own deaths. Neither beasts nor gods, mortals dwell and find their home in that bounded space between the "laws of the earth" and the "justice of the heavens" (*Antigone* 368–369).[6]

But what is it that constitutes this "in betweenness"? For that surely will be what is most strange about this strangest of beings. In one dense elliptic line in the very middle of the ode, Sophocles takes a stab at an answer: "And speech and wind-swift thought and law-abiding assemblies he has learnt."[7] It is, then, the power of speech, particularly the thoughtful speech of citizens gathered together in lawful assembly, that constitutes the wonderful strangeness of mortals. In what is surely a Sophoclean refrain, Isocrates declared that it is by the power of persuasive speech that we "are raised above the level of beasts, founded cities, laid down laws and discovered arts."[8]

However, whether in Argos or Thebes, San Salvador or Bosnia, the beast is, unfortunately, never far from the gate of the city and often roams in disguise within it. Still, it is strangely true that we do not always deal with each other as violent predators but, sometimes at least, as fellow citizens. If it is painfully evident that we humans are not a choir of angels, it is equally undeniable that neither are we a pack of wolves.

Sophocles' masterful ode and the theme of man's strangeness deserves more thorough consideration than these brief comments; but they are, I trust, sufficient for my point. By pointing to the ontological dimension which lies behind and grounds our civil discourse, I have located the perspective from which we can view the familiar ability to speak, to argue, to give an account of ourselves. It is the inexhaustibly rich but utterly strange phenomenon of our own humanity. And so, to discourse in the measured tones of the *civilis conversatio* is for us mortals to simply be what we ought to be. To tamper, to manipulate, to destroy that fragile dialogue is a barbarism that threatens and violates not only our civility but our very humanity itself: "*Si non es civis, non es homo*" (Remigio de Girolami).[9]

Public and Private Discourse

Remigio's forceful formulation might evoke a reasonable objection. Surely, in our times, *civic* discourse is not the only nor even the most significant speech mode that is constitutive of our humanity. That objection is worthy of consideration if for no other reason than that by contrasting civil discourse with different but equally "familiar" modes of speech, a second access into the otherness of the *civilis conversatio* might be opened up for us. If the *Antigone* ode offered us an initial vertical look at the strangeness of speech in the deeper wonder of our humanity, consideration of various types of human discourse—a horizontal view if you will—could provide an enlightening contrast to the idiosyncratic nature of civic speech. A number of possibilities come to mind here; for example, the theoretical language of the academy or the practical intercourse of the market-place. For my purpose, however, a more instructive contrast, since it is often confused with public speech, would be the private, intimate conversation of friends and lovers. In an age that trumpets on the open rooftops what ought to be shared in the privacy of the bedroom, it is refreshing to hear that old and wise commentator on public life, John Courtney Murray, delineate by way of contrast with private conversation the distinctive characteristics of public rhetoric. Dependent as it is on a respectful civility, public conversation lacks the frank, uninhibited interchange that occurs among close friends. Employing as it does reasoned argument, it is distinct from the intimate relation of husband and wife, for while "the marital relationship may at times be quarrelsome, . . . it is not argumentative." And based as public argument is on "reason, justice or power," it cannot share the "cordial warmth" of parental exchange, characterized as that is by "kinship, love and *pietas*."[10] (Wonderfully perceptive remarks, I might add, from someone who as a celibate was something of a stranger to married life.) In sum, the distinctive "climate of the city," Father Murray argues, "is not feral or familial but forensic. . . . It is cool and dry, with the coolness and dryness that characterizes good argument among reasoned men."[11]

This distinction between public and private discourse is so important because it cuts both ways, at once sheltering our intimate conversations from the harsh glare of publicity and opening for public exposure the common concerns of citizens. Unfortunately, there is no dearth of examples when it comes to the confusion of the two modes of discourse. I know a colleague who insists on having her students in a large public class on sexuality give out the private names they have for intimate parts of the body. A "liberating" experience no doubt! And one is reminded of President Johnson's exposing his scars to an embarrassed public or even President Carter's well-intentioned but inappropriate addressing as his "good friend" anyone whom he had ever met, even if only once. While they do reveal the pervasive extent of this rhetorical and political confusion, these illustrations are trivial when compared with the practice of conducting in dark and subversive ways what ought to be a public debate—the FBI under Hoover, the Nixon plumbers, and the Iran scandal come immediately to mind here. When these obfuscations become commonplace, an even more insidious result occurs. The suspicion is fostered that the public argument is merely ephemeral, always masking deeper, private wishes. Such subordination of public to private eviscerates the substance of public issues and eventually transforms the public debate into cynical propaganda. And once we have moved in that direction—where the public play is but a mask for our darker private desires—the human space where mortals dwell becomes dimmed and the turn toward violence and domination has been effected, almost unawares.

The Beasts Within

Up to this point I have attempted to develop an understanding of civil discourse by identifying it in its otherness, by distinguishing it, as it were, from without—from the complete destruction of it in violent anarchies, ancient and modern, to the mere absence of it in familial discourse. Now I would like to execute a more difficult trope: to illuminate the wonderful strangeness of our *civilis conversatio* from within, by distinguishing its mere appearances from the genuine article. While more difficult to ferret out, these simulacra of public discourse need to be identified if only so that we might appreciate all the more this tenuous, gossamer gift of reasoned speech, this very emblem of our humanity.

The barbarity which threatens civil discourse from within is less easily exposed because, as Father Murray so colorfully noted, the barbarian "need not appear in bearskins with a club in hand." Rather, "he may wear a Brooks Brothers suit and carry a ballpoint pen with which to write his advertising copy." In fact, "even beneath the academic gown there may lurk a child of the wilderness, untutored in the tradition of civility."[12] If Aristotle is correct that "the character of a speaker is the most powerful means of persuasion," then a rhetoric of salesmanship that serves naked self-interest and greed is surely most dangerous.[13] When selling the president becomes, as a practice, no different from selling any product, then

civil discourse is a mere guise that masks the image maker's manipulation of the public.

Unmasking the Brooks Brothers barbarian in all his myriad dis-
guises would be an intriguing if endless project; however, I would
rather pick up on the second of Murray's images: the feral child
hidden beneath an academic gown and the threat he or she presents
to reasoned discourse. Masked in the disarming disguise of tolerance,
the academic relativist and, to a lesser extent, the pluralist present
subtle but no less dangerous threats to our public civility than the barbarian with naked club in hand. When we follow these Janus-faced
twins back to their den, we will find a picture of humanity not unlike
the one we found in Argos and El Salvador and utterly alien from
Sophocles' *homo politicus* who speaks in "law-abiding assemblies."

Relativism

An anecdote might help us gain access into the mind of today's
relativist. The startling ignorance of history on the part of today's
students was recently and most charmingly illustrated by the question a very skeptical but earnest student asked at the end of what I
thought was a penetrating analysis of Thomas Aquinas's argument
on suicide. "This Aquinas fella," he queried, "was he before or after
Jesus?" Now some theologians might try to redeem (alas, all too
sanguinely) the young man's question by arguing that he demonstrated an inchoate sense of *kairos* even if his understanding of
chronos was a bit shaky. What intrigues me, however, is that the same
students who might on a matching test correlate "Caesar" and
"salad" are positively eloquent in their defense of the relativity of
historical truth. The very students who unabashedly proclaim their
disregard for history become, in the wink of an eye, the ardent
champions of historicism.

Such patent inconsistency might be excused on the premise that
young minds, rebellious of tradition and its perceived dogmatism,
are yet still uncertain of their own way in intellectual discourse. So
it would not be particularly worrisome that they would wear the
protective mask of relativism, except for the fact that I suspect
young students, good imitators that they are, have learned to repeat

what they have heard from their instructors. The climate of today's academy is decidedly relativistic. In some ways, that too is not so unexpected. Given the nature of the academy and the paramount importance of free and unrestricted debate, liberal educators have long stood watch at liberty's gates, courageously battling the foes of dogmatism and autocratic power that threaten our freedom of inquiry. But perhaps they may have stood watch so long and battled so fiercely that now they do damage in another direction. A new front has opened and they still battle on an old one that, if not won, has at least been temporarily secured. To use still another battle metaphor: while barring the front door of the *polis* against dogmatism, they have allowed the beast of relativism to creep almost unnoticed in the back door.[14]

Someone might immediately object that, while I need not agree with relativism, there is no need to characterize it as beastly or barbaric. My *ad hominem* attack does seem to suffer in contrast to the sweet tolerance of the relativist, who, in denying that there is any universal truth, accords each individual truth an equal status with every other truth. But if the definition of a barbarian is someone who does not live according to the rule of law, then barbaric speech is discourse that recognizes no reasoned or common linguistic standards. Yet that is precisely what relativism is: the rejection of any universal and binding rules of discourse. In its grip, the speaker is hopelessly trapped in a solipsistic universe where words mean only what one says they mean and truth is whatever one wants it to be. So, in effect, it is the relativist who is revealed as intolerant because, in foregoing all appeals to the persuasive character of truth, the speaker must rely on the only weapons left to effect one's purpose, the weapons of manipulation and violence. I think that is what Professor William Miller was getting at when he wrote: "Dogmatism is not the world's only danger, a moral vacuum is a danger, too, and a more pertinent one today, and curiously can turn into its apparent opposite."[15] From a logical point of view, it is rather easy to refute relativism, at least in the familiar, unsophisticated version one hears bandied about in today's culture. In fact, that relativism is self-refuting because every affirmation of the truth that all truth is relative is, of course, self-contradictory or, in the philosophical jargon, performatively inconsistent. While logic is a legitimate ground of appeal and no little comfort to reasoned persons, unfortunately the cultural climate often seems impervious to its necessities.[16] I find when I trot out the argument from self-reference against my relativist colleagues, the response is invariably: "Oh, yeah, if you want to use logic . . ." Now, putting aside the obvious rejoinder ("Well, what is it that you want to use?") and, again, fully mindful that the rejection of logic itself assumes it, we cannot deny the very real existential thrust of relativism today. As a rejoinder to that entrenched but often unexamined cultural bias, the logical riposte causes only a surface wound. We need to cut deeper into the very lineaments of our public speech to test the concrete compatibility of the relativist's claim. For a start, let us return to the commonplace world of classroom discussion.

Strangely enough, it often happens that the same students who trumpet relativism can be found, only a few classes later, locked in argument over abortion or capital punishment or the use of military force in the Middle East. It is as though the natural, human drive to speak and debate about what is true and false erupts from within them and shatters the thick veneer of relativism. Quickly forgotten is the foppish cant about "what's good for you may not be good for me," replaced instead by a passionate exchange over what is right and wrong. And that exchange is predicated upon a two-fold dialectic: truth that is at once authoritative and elusive, and judgment that is tentative yet inescapable.[17] Any *real* argument must assume a truth that is yet to be fully uncovered and a rightness of action that can be anticipated and evaluated. Why else would we argue?

A hardened relativist might reply that what seems to be a reasoned debate about what is true and good is, in reality, nothing more than self-display or devious manipulation to achieve one's own ends.[18] Such a "hermeneutic of suspicion" (to use Paul Ricoeur's phrase) is a rather accurate account of what sometimes occurs in the rhetorical transaction. But to reduce all rhetoric to either naked or disguised self-interest is to cut against the grain of our experience that leads us to posit, for example, the distinction between persuasion and propaganda, between what we care about and what we are simply interested in. The only stratagem left to the practitioner of this suspicious hermeneutic is the endless unmasking of "good intentions." But in this flattened rhetorical landscape, the unmasker still tries to be as persuasive as possible. Even the hermeneutic of suspicion must claim its own suspicion as truth.

The upshot of my argument thus far can be stated as follows: if we pay close attention to the fabric of our rhetoric, we cannot fail to see the inescapable datum that truth lies as a necessary condition behind all our linguistic transactions. Our hypocrisies, even our lies, bear witness to the truth we are trying to dissimulate or deny. Elusive it may well be, but that only makes the truth more seductive.[19]

The onslaught of relativism does, then, have one beneficial effect. It has forced us to look again at our familiar public speech acts and see them, strangely enough, as they really are. This is no mean feat, given that the history of rhetoric is replete with examples of interpreters, from Sophists to Deconstructionists, who would translate public speech into a language other than its own. Critical to this mistranslation is the tendency to see rhetoric as nothing more than an instrumental activity, the ultimate meaning of which lies outside—either before or after—the speech itself. There are those (often, unfortunately, philosophers) who would reduce rhetoric to a means chosen to effect a purpose that is chosen prior to the rhetorical situation. In this rhetoric of intentions, a speaker might first decide on the truth of a matter and then choose various rhetorical devices (stories and metaphors, for example) to communicate the truth to a less enlightened public. But this viewpoint fails to take into account the essential reality of public discourse, which involves a reciprocal transaction between speaker and audience. Usually, the intention or purpose does come first chronologically. Phenomenologically and ontologically, however—that is, from the perspective of the act itself—it is the public discourse that is prior because the intention is but an anticipation of the public act and finds its fulfillment (if it is a good speech) in that public act. The speech act is not a separate event, much less a philosophical afterthought from a prior intention; but rather, the intention is embodied in the rhetorical situation. Similarly, there are those (often communication arts specialists) who would locate the meaning of the rhetorical act in the consequences of the speech. So, a good speech is what results in the right or intended effect. Again, we are confronted with an instrumental view of rhetoric that eviscerates the public, objective reality of the speech itself. If public discourse is a neutral act justified only in terms of its consequences, then we would have to dismiss as "bad rhetoric" most of Isocrates, some of Cicero's greatest speeches, and that most beautiful of all public discourses, the *Apology* of Socrates. Consequences are always consequences *of* . . . and that "of" reveals the derivative nature of consequences; that is, they do not determine but rather flow from the thing itself, which, in this case, is our shared public discourse.[20] I can, even today, still hear ringing in my ears an old Latin teacher's monition: "Things are what they are and their consequences will be what they will be."

Pluralism

Might it not be, however, that in our passionate efforts to avoid the vortex of relativism we tack too far leeward, floundering on the shoals of dogmatism? Even if we grant the philosopher his unrelenting (and often unrequited) search for truth, is it not more prudent to assume that no single Truth can dominate the domain of action? How many careers and even lives have been needlessly sacrificed on the altar of some supposed truth? The highly influential contemporary rhetorician Chaim Perelman worried that, when dogmatists "do not succeed in persuading everyone of their point of view, they may justify coercion and the use of force against the recalcitrants in the name of God, of reason, of truth, or of the state's or party's interest."[21] By contrast, Perelman argued, a pluralistic state would foster competing interest groups and ideologies, encourage their interchange, all the while resolutely remaining above the fray, impartially "maintain[ing] a balance" and "moderating their most dangerous excesses" (p. 67). By offering a model of the good society which places a premium on tolerance and liberty, pluralism seems a likely candidate to cut between the twin evils of relativism and dogmatism. "Only pluralism," Perelman claims, "can save us from idolatry" (p. 80).

Before we become too familiar with the pluralist's claim, however, we need to inspect it more carefully; for that, we turn particularly to Professor Perelman's eloquent defense of it, since he is a rhetorician of enormous stature and, more importantly, because he believes that only within the fertile soil of pluralism can the rhetoric of our civil discourse bloom and prosper.

Interestingly enough, Perelman's adoption of a pluralistic model of discourse comes only after he laid aside his earlier espousal of positivism with its corresponding belief in the relativity of all moral judgments. While he continued to maintain, along with the positivists, that value judgments "could be neither the result of experience nor the logical consequence of incontestable principles," he still came to believe that these value judgments (far from being arbitrary) are embedded in our public discourse and contain within themselves certain canons of practical reasonableness.[22] These rationality norms (for example, the rule of justice which dictates each person be given his due) do not spring from universal truths about the world but, to the extent that they are invariant, are purely formal or tautological. Nonetheless, they do provide the speaker and his audience with some criteria by which the efficacy of public discourse might be judged. Does income redistribution, for instance, give each person his or her due? Within these canons, Perelman often reiterated, it was certainly possible that two or more competing viewpoints—much like Kantian antinomies—could clash and no further rational judgment about their superiority would be possible. One could imagine two distinct tax systems, both of which appeal to rational but divergent views of what constitutes justice. His championing of a moral and political pluralism becomes, then, a natural objective correlate of his model of practical reason. In the same way, there are no ultimate political truths save those formal rules of operation which legitimize public debate and those procedural rules which specify how issues are to be resolved fairly and equitably. If that leaves things rather "vague," Perelman reminds us that politics is not an exact science and, besides, a "respect for diversity" implies a situational approach that requires a "sensitivity to all existing values" (p. 67).

A familiar analogy suggests itself here—one that is often employed by pluralists themselves—and that is the analogy of an athletic contest. In most games, for example, the referees or umpires perform a function similar to the state's in the pluralistic model. They guard against violations of the rules and ensure the smooth running of the game, and in all this they must remain scrupulously impartial, leaving the game's outcome to athletic superiority and, to a certain extent, fate. The analogy is indeed suggestive, even more so than pluralists are, I think, willing to admit, concentrating as they do almost exclusively on the role of the referee. To really understand the game, however, one must comprehend the rules and how they foster—or possibly detract from—the excellence of the play. Further, and most crucially for our purposes, one can ask why the two teams play at all. Surely the purposes for which they play—for fun or for money, for example—determine the meaning of the game, and we might judge which purposes are more in keeping with the nature of the sport. Hence, two teams which share a common purpose will most likely create a better atmosphere of play than two teams with conflicting or hostile purposes. Finally, is it not the purpose of league commissioners and representatives to ensure what they call the "integrity of the game"? We could go on, but the point is, I think, clear. The reality of sport, like the reality of our civic life, is much richer and demands more of a common purpose than the merely procedural consensus of the pluralist model allows.

At this point, we need to distinguish between pluralism as a theoretical legitimation of the umpire view of the state and the phenomenon of diverse, pluralistic groups operating within the context of a political system. The latter is hardly objectionable; indeed, they have formed, as Tocqueville insightfully noted, the bedrock of our American political tradition. The tradition of religious pluralism, for example, is certainly one of the richest fruits of our Constitutional heritage. But, as the example of athletics demonstrated, it is important to ask *why* such a pluralistic arrangement is *good* for our common civic life. What purpose does it serve? That question is hardly moot since political thinkers and actors—pluralists included—have recognized the inherent tension and even danger created by competing and conflicting groups operating within a society.[23] Here, pluralism as an ideology offers little enlightenment. Beyond some rather superficial and historically inaccurate claims about America's "liberal traditions," moral and political justification appears rather thin. At times, pluralists seem to display a charming but thoroughly discredited faith in an invisible hand guiding the competing allegiances to a harmonious and happy outcome. Perelman's defense is not that naive; yet, ultimately, it is far more insidious. He has no illusions about the conflicts that will irrupt in a pluralistic society. He envisions the emergence of new "Antigones," rebels whose consciences will be formed by a "social pluralism" in which the individual's identity transcends any group identity (p. 65). For not only will groups be in competition, but the same individual will have memberships in these diverse, even conflicting organizations. In such a crucible, Perelman believes, the autonomous individual will be molded, whose substantial worth is over and above the somewhat insubstantial political order, the purpose of which is to protect that individual's freedom. Yet, on one count at least, the political is superior to the individual, in the stark fact that the former holds a "monopoly of the use of force." That control is what keeps these autonomous individuals and conflicting groups from each other's throats. Despite Perelman's attempt to give this account of political beginnings a classical ring, his thought owes less to the *koinōphilia* of Aeschylus's *Eumenides* and Sophocles' *Antigone* and much more to those modern thinkers, like Hobbes and Weber, who see the state's power as the sole check on individuals' insatiable appetites. Substituting the referee for Hobbes's absolute sovereign creates at least the illusion of mitigated state power; but, in Perelman's model, only the state's capacity to stand for anything, not its actual control, remains unchecked. One shudders to think what rough beast might slouch into that vacuum.[24]

Though decidedly more civilized, there are still strong vestiges of that old barbarism, relativism, in this version of pluralism. Perelman, for example, is fond of using illustrations of judicial decisions where what was thought just and even reasonable in one age is judged unjust and unreasonable in another. His favorite example is the Belgium Supreme Court's reversal in 1922 of a ruling in 1889 that prohibited women from practicing law for the reason (as stated in the 1889 ruling) that it was a "truism too obvious . . . that the administration of justice was reserved for men" (p. 68). Yesterday's truism is today's fallacy. But Perelman misses the point, and his discussion seems surprisingly insensitive to the actual rhetorical debate that surrounds arguments about rights. Yesterday's truism is rejected not because it is no longer au courant (should women's *rights* go in and out of style?) but because what seemed a truism then has been proven, through debate over time, to be *wrong*. No mere procedural consensus can lead us to that conclusion; rather, only the thoughtful recognition that political rights, when given to some, must be given to all. Undeniably, there will always be a sort of bandwagon effect, but the political debate, unless it has degenerated into mere self-advertisement, appeals to our sense of right and wrong, justice and injustice. Even the fact, noted earlier, that two competing actions or policies might both be equally just does not entail, as Perelman claims, a relativistic or even formalistic notion of justice. Justice is not the name of an ethereal thing but rather a principle which, in guiding our actions, leaves a fair amount of room for maneuverability and even ingenuity. But as a substantive understanding of what it means to be fair to others, it is not just a formal, arbitrarily defined concept either. Perelman is right when he asserts with Aristotle that there can be no a priori deductive science of politics, but he is quite un-Aristotelian when he assumes the only alternative is to banish Truth or Justice from the borders of the *polis*. What else is Aristotle's notion of practical reason but the attempt, albeit often uncertain, to determine the right thing to do at the right time and in the right way.

Relativism wanted us to accept as true the inconsistent claim that there is no truth. Perelman's pluralism would have us believe that a good society is one in which no ultimate good is allowed to rule. Pluralism leaves us without the civilizing garment of a common creed. Cast in the naked role of combatants (only a few can be umpires), we endlessly and aggressively pursue our own autonomous interest over against the good of others.

If, on the other hand, we are to transcend this naked struggle of interests and build, in Professor Miller's words, "a common life" based on "a meaningful civic argument," then we must hold to certain public truths that express who we are and what we stand for. Curiously enough, in one of his essays, published in English after his death, Perelman himself seemed to recognize the need for a common body of truths, although in a qualified way. Without a common devotion to values, Perelman argued, there can be no political community.

> It is this devotion which unites the members of such a community, which permits it to surmount the passing crises, the discords over secondary problems and the personal conflicts which never fail to surface in all human groups where members maintain between themselves multiple and durable relations.[25]

He even goes as far as to say that "ultimately these extolled values will be considered to be absolute, sacred, untouchable and even indisputable."[26] The tone of these remarks, coming from the same thinker who but a few years earlier had denounced the dictatorial monism of those who affirmed universal values, is, at the very least, quite striking. However, these thoughts emerge within the context of analysis of epideictic discourse where the orator's task is "the enhancement of values" already held rather than dialectic discourse where, for Perelman, the orator's task is to question and challenge. Furthermore, Perelman seems particularly careful to qualify every mention of universal values with such phrases as "devoted to . . ." or "considered to be . . ." universal and absolute.[27] Perelman's hedging leaves us, unfortunately, with but one more simulacrum of civic discourse. An epideictic discourse which espouses universal values serves only an instrumental function; that is, its goodness is judged by how well it molds and sustains a community. It reminds one of those nonreligious thinkers who hail religious values for their stabilizing—or, often in today's rhetoric, revolutionary—effect. In such cynicism we encounter, once again, the "hermeneutic of suspicion." The danger in this pragmatism (a danger Perelman seems blissfully ignorant of) is that, if values are solely instrumental, then like any tools they can and should be replaced when more efficient ones are developed. Surely there are more effective, if barbarous, ways of keeping people together than rhetorical appeals! But, as I pointed out earlier, appeals to solidarity, freedom, justice—or any value, for

that matter—reflect the way we see and interpret our actual transactions with one another. If, for example, I were to betray my
country—even if it were to lead to the good effect of creating heroic
and successful patriots—that consequence would in no way
diminish my act of betrayal.[28] If no name for my betrayal existed, we
would surely have to invent one to describe what humans can do,
and at times *do* do, to one another. To reiterate my argument in
chapter 2: the common consensus that could truly knit a community together cannot be an ideological overlay but must be
embedded in the very sinews of our relationships with one another.
Again, it was Murray who exposed modernity's attempt to reduce
the public good to something less than it really is.

> The consensus is not a structure of secondary rationaliza-
> tions erected on psychological data (as the behaviorist
> would have it) or on economic data (as the Marxist would
> have it). It is not the residual minimum left after rigid appli-
> cation of the Cartesian axiom, "*de omnibus dubitandum.*" It is
> not simply a set of working hypotheses whose value is prag-
> matic. It is an ensemble of substantive truths, a structure of
> basic knowledge, an order of elementary affirmations that
> reflect realities inherent in the order of existence.[29]

I doubt Perelman would accept that, but I know of no other way to
avoid what he himself calls "the sordid struggle of opposing self-
interest" which leads to "a return of barbarism."[30]

Consensus and a Disputed Case

Against the familiar backdrop of pluralism and its minimalistic
interpretation of civic discourse, the real nature of our public speech
has, at long last, come into focus. Only within the walls of some
shared truths and common values can civic discourse be at home
and flourish. Some thinkers, the "early" Perelman among them,
seem to think that affirming universal truths and values can only
spell the death of argument. But that is an ill-conceived notion. "It
seems to have been one of the corruptions of intelligence by posi-

tivism," Murray wrote, "to assume that argument ends when agreement is reached. In a basic sense, the reverse is true. There can be no argument except on the premise, and within a context, of agreement."[31] That we have achieved some success in allowing for the flourishing of disagreement within the context of consensus is what George Weigel has appropriately called the "miracle" of the American experiment. His words are worth quoting at length:

> For the fact remains that, with one terrible break, the United States has formed and sustained political community amidst luxuriant plurality for over two centuries. We are a multiracial people. On the street corner of any major city and most sizable towns one finds churches, a synagogue, and, latterly, a mosque. We are conservatives and neo-conservatives, liberals and neo-liberals, radicals, libertarians, and agrarian populists. We disagree, often passionately, on virtually every item on the public agenda. We live in, and wish to be accountable to, many communities: family, religious community, political party, voluntary association. Yet we are, in the midst of it all, a *political* community that has settled its arguments about the public ordering of our lives, loves, and loyalties without organized mass violence since 1865.
>
> This is no mean accomplishment.[32]

But that fragile consensus, when it exists, is usually implicit, often obscured in the complexity of events, even willfully contemned in the heat of partisan exchange and so continually in danger of being lost. For that reason, the public consensus must itself from time to time become the theme rather than the premise of the public argument. Perhaps an extended example might reveal how that consensus must be hammered out anew.

Much of the public debate that has occupied center stage for at least the last four decades in the American polity has centered around the issue of violence and its justification. From the civil rights movement and the Vietnam conflict to intervention in Latin America, the Middle East, and Bosnia, events have compelled us to confront whether or not and to what extent force could ever be justified in the public arena. Though the public record fairly bristles with acrimonious debate, even to the casual observer it is clear that very little authentic civil argument is occurring. The reason is that the debate lies not with these specific issues—what George Weigel calls the "binary options" of "for and against"—but with a deeper or "contextual" level where "moral imagination and moral reasoning make their primary claim and offer the most salient counsel."[33] At that level, there are a number of conflicting assumptions that bear scrutiny, but here I wish to focus on an old debate that stirs now in a new skin, pacifism versus just-war theory. Though the number of Americans who would describe themselves as pacifists is still a distinct minority, the threat of nuclear holocaust has given new credence to pacifist categories, and pacifism's rhetorical impact certainly has transcended its relatively small number of street adherents.[34] Against the moral vision of pacifism stands the just-war theory, the more traditional way of giving a moral account of the use of violence, an account that today is often under severe attack from pacifists and militarists who are highly suspicious whether its categories can deal with the realities of modern warfare.

Suspicions aside, it is these two moral viewpoints that animate many of the actors in the political debate, and because their assumptions are at such cross-purposes the debate usually ends in a hopeless impasse. Just how irreconcilable both views seem to be is evidenced in the mutual rejection of each other's fundamental option. The pacifist rejects the starting point of the just-war theory, that human life may be taken in a just cause. Conversely, just-war theorists cannot accept the fundamental credal proposition of the pacifist, that killing is always wrong. For the pacifist, just-war theory begins with an untenable and immoral belief that killing can be justified and acceptable limits placed on violence. For the just-war theorist, pacifism's inefficacious response to evil is at best suspect and, when urged against a nation's fundamental right of self-defense, it becomes patently immoral. No common moral turf seems possible for these combatants. Absent that common ground, the moral sincerity and seriousness of purpose of the proponents tend only to exacerbate, rather than moderate, the disagreement.

Charges and countercharges of moral blindness and turpitude too often fill the air. A rather vicious circle is constructed whereby the argument begins at the level of a specific policy (for example, the use of force against Iraq), then moves of necessity to the level of conflicting assumptions; but since these are irreconcilable, the debate must return to the original issue—only now the disputants are no longer "locked in argument" but must utilize naked power and manipulative rhetoric to carry the day and win over an often confused citizenry. Admittedly, describing the conflict in such a way does not do justice to some of the shadings of the argument, but anyone who has listened to the ongoing strident debate can at least sense the absence of the *civilis conversatio*.

If the deadlock could be broken and an authentic civil argument were to be made possible, what would have to occur? First of all, a bit of ground clearing (or "rhetorical hermeneutic," if you will) might profitably be employed. Rather than serving as admittedly diverse ways of understanding our public interactions, the categories of just war and pacifism often function as ideological cudgels in the arsenals of conservatives and liberals respectively. By contrast, an authentic rhetoric would call upon the just-war theorist to place himself or herself under the strictures of the just-war argument in order to discern, for example, whether or not violent intervention in a particular case is justified. Such a strategic commitment might prove illuminating and certainly a welcome antidote to the *ex post facto* rationalizations that are often offered to justify American intervention, as for example in Grenada. By the same token, a pacifist response to the Sandinistas' repression of freedom might well have been a call for militant nonviolent resistance instead of the usual ideological calls for solidarity with the "revolutionary" front.[35] What is important here is not logical consistency for its own sake but a certain intellectual honesty that reveals a willingness to follow an argument to its appropriate (even if unwanted) conclusion. That does happen at times in the public debate, if infrequently. I can remember vividly hearing Eugene McCarthy in the late 1960s deliver one of his first public pronouncements against the Vietnam War in a packed Washington church. Instead of fire-and-brimstone denunciations of America (clearly what many in the audience wanted to hear), he gave a long and painstaking analysis of American involvement, judging it according to the categories of the just-war tradition. The impression left with me was that of a conscientious senator's anguished appraisal of acts that, given his preference, he would not have liked to—but was forced to—call immoral. Similarly—whether one agrees with them or not—that same willingness to subject one's principles to moral realities occurs when Nat Henthoff, a liberal with impeccable credentials, opposes abortion and that staunch conservative George Will condemns capital punishment. Between the completely predictable ideologue and the chameleonlike opportunist stand reflective and committed citizens who continually surprise us with fresh insights.

Secondly, attention must be paid to these underlying, contextual assumptions. The fact that the disputed question: "Ought human life ever be taken?" is so little argued in today's forums indicates, I fear, a dreadful lacuna in the public argument about war and peace.[36] Were the argument to center on the moral logic of self-defense, a number of interesting questions would force themselves onto center stage. Among them:

1. In killing another in self-defense do we not thereby treat life as an instrumental, not an intrinsic, good?

2. Does it make moral sense to say that in war we directly intend our nation's defense and only accept but not directly intend the death of the enemy?

3. Is the pacifist principle *"vita servanda, ruat coelum"* ("let life be preserved, though the heavens fall") a defensible stance?

4. What *is* the appropriate response to evil in the world?

Granted, these questions do not easily lend themselves to the give and take of most public forums. They strike deeper than the binary options mentioned earlier; indeed they do not lead to answers in the traditional sense of that word. But therein lies their power: they cut behind partisan allegiances and invite the participants into a more reflective posture. While it does not mean abandonment of one's fundamental principles, to think about these questions or, better, to agree to think about these questions together does imply a willingness to distance oneself for a while from the heat of the battle and to engage in a real dialogue. Such civil conversations about fundamental principles, while not common, are certainly not without precedent. The ecumenical dialogue among American churches serves as a striking reminder that reflection on deeply held beliefs can lead to a deeper appreciation of shared commitments and a more profound understanding of disagreements.[37]

Civil conversation that attends to these underlying assumptions could lead, thirdly, to a fashioning of a consensus upon which a renewed public debate might commence. The advocates of both positions do, after all, share a vision of the public world that is *moral*. While that may seem little more than tautological, we should recall Aristotle's comment about the importance of a starting point and how often it is missed because it is so obvious.[38] If advocates of both positions offer us distinctly moral visions, that does distinguish them from those who would deny that moral categories can be applied to issues of war and peace (the "war is hell" and "all is fair" bluster) and those for whom the only consideration is a self-serving one (the "nothing is worth dying for" cant). At least both pacifism and just-war theory, in the words of the Roman Catholic Bishops' Pastoral, "seek to serve the common good."[39] Given the contemporary rejection of any notion of a common good, that agreement, though it often goes unrecognized, should not be underestimated.

Furthermore, the shared consensus has, I believe, some substantive content. Both positions begin with a moral presumption against war—that is obvious in the pacifist case, but the limiting conditions of the just-war theory (only, for example, as a last resort and with some hope of success) imply a prima facie case against the use of lethal violence. In other words, the burden of proof, the just-war theorist recognizes, lies with those who would resort to violence. Both positions then accept the implied sanction in moral structures: there are some things which just ought not be done no matter what. They each draw the line at a different juncture but draw it they do—the pacifist will not take human life no matter what; the just-war theorist will not directly intend the killing of innocent human beings, no matter what.[40]

What occasions the response of justified violence or militant nonviolence can also be a moral assessment that is shared. However one chooses to oppose totalitarian aggression, clearly the pacifist and just-war theorist share a similar revulsion against this abasement of humanity. Again, Gandhi and our revolutionary founders chose different methods to deal with British colonialism, but both responses were occasioned by the moral assessment of a violated liberty. Interestingly enough, the fact that pacifists and just-war theorists can share a moral assessment of a regime independent of their positions on taking human life can also help explain why they can forge alignments other than the just-war and pacifist ones. Pacifists and just-war theorists may differ among themselves about their assessment of the regimes in Latin America or the Middle East. So one can imagine not only a just-war theorist with liberal leanings but even a pacifist with conservative views. That makes the sorting out of the debate all the more difficult but certainly no less interesting.

Fourthly, dialogue that accepted and probed these shared assumptions might well transform the sometimes acerbic denunciation from both sides into affirmations of some common virtues. The tendency within pacifist circles to assume a self-righteous, even fanatical, purity of conscience and among just-war theorists to adopt a disdainful, even arrogant, attitude of realpolitik could be moderated by a common recognition of the courage and prudence demanded by both moral attitudes. Gandhi's admiration of the soldier's willingness to risk his life is an instructive example here, as is the noted pacifist Gordon Zahn's celebration of Hans Jägerstätter's conscientious opposition to Nazi military induction on the grounds of just-war theory. Common virtues reveal a common way of sizing up the world and entail, I think, a shared world of discourse.

It is one thing to search for the common ground that would allow two opposing positions to speak to one another. It is quite another thing to play the role of mediator. Any attempt to mediate these two great traditions runs the risk of failing, in Nietzsche's words, "to see the unparalleled" and ending up with not a mean but "the mediocre."[41] Nonetheless, let me suggest, finally, a practical modus operandi that allows for their conflicting premises while acknowledging their common ground. Permit me a bit of poetic license to adopt Keats's thoughtful and poignant metaphor of human life, "a large Mansion of Many Apartments" (which of course is itself an adaptation of the Gospel saying "In my Father's house there are many mansions").[42] In a somewhat whimsical way let me suggest we might accommodate, in Keats's mansion, both traditions in a way that nurtures each and allows the argument to continue. Rooms in our polity can be found for both: the just-war theory, because it entails the ethical base for self-defense, on the first floor perhaps, and pacifism, because of the sublimity of its vision, in the turret. Our political mansion must have a sprawling, Victorian look to it! Even so, there would have to be some "house rules" if their living together is not to constitute another one of those "uneasy truces" we spoke about it reference to the Bouvia case in chapter 2. An acceptance by each position of the moral legitimacy (not necessarily correctness and certainly not perfection) of the other would entail a willingness of both parties to tone down the rhetoric. Pacifism is not treason any more than just-war theory represents a pact with the devil of militarism. A willingness to take ourselves a good deal less seriously than the truths we seek to live by would surely go a long way in modulating a new rhetorical tone.

If the just-war theory represents a standard by which all must abide, the pacifist commitment to a life of total nonviolence might represent a vocation similar to what the Christian church has called the "evangelical counsels." Traditionally, these counsels or calls to perfection have been expressed in a religious community dedicated to poverty, chastity, and obedience. There is no reason why pacifist communities could not view themselves and be accepted by others as specially committed to a life of nonviolence. Communities of non-violence could stand in witness to the rest of us of the moral superiority of nonviolence in ordinary circumstances and a reminder, in the extraordinary cases when the state resorts to violence, of the boundaries and limitations of violence. Just as a community that witnesses to poverty reminds us of the temptations of wealth and the truth that the spirit is superior to the material, so a pacifist community might remind us of our obligation to always seek first the solution of nonviolence.

In the religious tradition, the evangelical counsels were never seen as a universal demand nor were they even seen as the only way to perfection. They represented rather a special calling to embody in a dramatic way the life of the spirit.[43] Their force became binding only upon one who freely took a vow to live by their directives. Adopting such a model would militate against a pacifist's self-righteousness on the one hand and, on the other, a just-war theorist's disdain for the ideal. An inherent tension would always exist between the two viewpoints, but it *could* be a creative one.[44] Surely a good *polis* has room enough for a Francis of Assisi and a Thomas More.

Lacking as I do the eloquent tongue of Athena, my efforts at reconciliation here may well have fallen short. But at least these efforts at persuasion might convince the reader that consensus is possible and the issue worth pursuing. "Confronted with an apparent stalemate, there is no need to give in to moral or intellectual 'pluralism,'" claims Ronald Beiner, "for it always remains open to say 'Press on with the arguments.'"[45] That the argument needs to be pressed today, on so many fronts, indicates how urgently we need a civic rhetoric and the citizens to speak it. According to Walter Lippmann, "perhaps the highest function of a public servant in a free and democratic society is to preserve its oneness as a community while he fights the battles which divide it."[46] Such a delicate task, as Lippmann fully knew, could only be accomplished within the framework of an authentic civic discourse. That *civilis conversatio*, operating as it must according to the *logos* of persuasion, tacking between the rocks of dogmatism and the eddies of relativism, respecting the freedom and equality of its listeners, and aiming at a justly ordered society, could truly create what Aristotle called *homonoia*, the "like-mindedness" of citizens who choose, judge, and execute all things in light of the common good.[47]

CHAPTER 5

Public Action: Rosa Parks and Two Very Old Dead White European Males

Thought, by itself, moves nothing.—Aristotle

Now is the time to move. This is no time to talk;
it is time to act.—Rev. L. Roy Bennett at organizational
meeting for the Montgomery bus boycott

Rosa Parks and Aristotle

D ecember 1, 1955, Thursday. Late afternoon in Montgomery, Alabama. A Negro seamstress by the name of Rosa Parks left work at the men's alteration department of Montgomery Fair, a popular store in the downtown area. After purchasing a few items across the street at the drugstore, she boarded the Cleveland Avenue bus (not knowing that, before she would reach home, her little odyssey would alter the course of American history). The back of the bus, the section designated for Negroes only, was filled.

In the middle section behind the "whites only" seats (popularly known as "no man's land") there was a single aisle seat. Rosa Parks sat down . . . and, as the song that commemorates the event records, "when Momma Parks sat down, the whole world stood up." But, again, Rosa Parks was not anticipating any such momentous event. She was just tired and, as she would remark later: "My feet hurt."

In talking about these events I have followed the practice of most historians in using the out-of-date term "Negro" to remain faithful as possible to the circumstances and to the language employed in those days.

According to the bus company's policy, the seats in between the Negro and white sections could be occupied by Negroes, but the bus driver had the option of making them available to whites if the white section was filled. When a white man got on the bus and had to stand, the bus driver called out to the Negroes in the first row behind the white section to let him have those seats. What happened next could be told with no more eloquence than by Mrs. Parks herself:

> At his first request, didn't any of us move. Then he spoke again and said, "You'd better make it light on yourselves and let me have those seats." . . . When the three people, the man who was in the seat with me and the two women [across the aisle] stood up and moved into the aisle, I remained where I was. When the driver saw that I was still sitting there, he asked if I was going to stand up. I told him, no I wasn't. He said, "Well, if you don't stand up, I'm going to have you arrested." I told him go on and have me arrested.[1]

He did. And that simple but heroic act of resistance sparked the Montgomery bus boycott, which in turn ignited the great civil rights movement of the late fifties and early sixties.[2]

I began this work on the public good with the example of Elizabeth Bouvia, whose defiant wish to end her life led me to characterize her as a modern Antigone. I conclude with the example of another woman, Rosa Parks, whose quiet act of resistance for the sake of a public good breaks the Antigone mold and expresses a new synthesis of individual and communal good, of morality and politics, that is worthy of the divine reconciler Athena herself. In a very real way, the fateful choice for public action today is: In whose footsteps will we follow, Elizabeth Bouvia's or Rosa Parks's?

This final chapter, then, will be a reflection on the nature of political action and its relation to the public good. No different than in Homer's day, what continues to characterize a human being as distinct from beasts and gods is the call to be a "speaker of words and a doer of deeds." Both. Speech without action is mere pretense, at best ineffectual, at worst hypocritical. And action demands an accounting (a *logos*) if it is to be understood and justified. To do just that—to render an account of action—let us return to the case of Rosa Parks, employing as our initial guide that very old and long dead white European male, Aristotle of Stagira. In his brilliant treatment of practical wisdom (*phronēsis*) in book 6 of the *Nichomachean Ethics*, he presents the theoretical context for Rosa Parks's heroic deed.

The facts surrounding the Rosa Parks events are important because, as Aristotle reminds us, human acts are particular things. Unlike theoretical knowledge, which he thinks aims at universal and necessary truths, deliberating about what one ought to do involves an acquaintance with the particular and the contingent. The fact that human beings can deliberate (*boulomai*) and make a choice (*proairesis*) among a number of different courses of action is another one of those distinguishing traits of human beings. Because human acts can be other than what they are, they are distinguishable from those instinctual behaviors of beasts who cannot act otherwise and the divine "activity" of purely speculative thought that proceeds by way of the necessary laws of logic.[3]

Rosa Parks could have done otherwise. Certainly she was given a choice by both the bus driver and, later, the policemen who came to arrest her. She could have made it "light on herself" and stood like the others. She also had time to deliberate not only in those anxious moments when the bus driver waited for her to move but in the considerably longer time when the driver went to summon the police. While her act possessed a certain stubborn spontaneity, it is clear from her own testimony that she had thought long and hard about the injustice of segregated buses and, indeed, had over a course of years more than once been thrown off the buses for refusing to abide by the practice of having Negroes pay in the front, then exit and reboard at the rear of the vehicle. Rosa Parks knew what she was doing.

But not only do we deliberate about particulars, the good that we do is a particular good. The human good, as I have reiterated throughout this work, is not relative (that is, contingent on whatever we want it to be) but it is particular (that is, specific to human beings). Even if some other animals could deliberate or possess some fore-sight—and Aristotle allows that might be possible (1141a28–30)—the particular good of a fish would be specific to it and distinct from a human being's good. I assume Aristotle is referring to such obvious phenomena as fish showing little inclination to leave the sea and humans' avowed preference for dry land or at least relatively unleaky boats. But I suspect he also has other, greater fish to fry.

Rosa Parks was acting on behalf of a specific human good, the good of justice. And justice here is not the law of the seas or the jungle—eat or be eaten—but the human mandate to treat each person fairly and equitably.[4] We do not blame sharks for eating other, more vulnerable fish. We do condemn as unjust forcing African Americans (or any group) to crowd in the back of the bus solely because of the color of their skin. The Sophists of Socrates' day were wont to argue that the law of nature as evidenced in the animal kingdom dictated that might makes right. It has been the view of more noble souls from Socrates to Rosa Parks that human justice requires otherwise.

So, Rosa Parks acted out of a moral mandate, but that alone is insufficient to judge her act as right, much less great. Had she moved to the back of the bus we would hardly have condemned her, any more than she condemned the three who did. In fact, many people at the time (and not all of them whites) thought her act foolish or imprudent. How, then, might we come to understand what makes public acts good, given the fact that the very contingent nature of such acts prohibits the application of any rigid formula to judge their correctness? To tackle that question we need to look a bit more closely at Aristotle's definition of that virtue which guides action: practical wisdom.

Practical Wisdom—Defined

Put simply, practical wisdom (*phronesis*) is knowing what to do. But knowing what to do, as most of us realize, does not come naturally. It is an acquired disposition that comes only with practice. Greek writers (Homer, Aeschylus, Aristotle—to name a few) liked to use archery as a metaphor for doing the right thing. Hitting the target, neither too high nor too low, neither wide left nor wide right, was much like the aim of action, to hit the mean between excess and deficiency. And just as the archer must learn how to "stretch and relax his bow" (6.1138b23) according to where the target is and the archer's own height and weight, so the actor must learn to do the right thing by adjusting his or her particular character to the particular situation. Virtue, of course, is more than just a skill like archery, but they both demand the same thing: practice, practice, practice. That is not a popular prescription today. We seem particularly susceptible to the Socratic fallacy that knowing the good will lead quite naturally to doing the good. At any rate, Aristotle is more sober and, alas, more realistic. To be good, one must do good. Indeed, he went so far as to say that "some people without knowledge (*eidotes*) are better at acting than those with knowledge, especially the experienced ones" (6.1141b17–19).

Now Rosa Parks was a seamstress, not a theoretician. But she was experienced in the evils of segregation and she did know what needed to be done. Wise she certainly was, but it was a wisdom born of experience, what Aristotle called "practical." In a telling remark, this man who invented the ultimate theoretical science— metaphysics—suggested that if we could only have one type of wisdom—theoretical or practical—it is better to have the latter (6.1141b22–23). Spike Lee has got it; it *is* more important to "do the right thing." In the early days of the civil rights movement, many citizens, some well intentioned, urged efforts at changing the hearts of segregationists rather than changing the laws. Martin Luther King used to have a trenchant response to that view. While he thought it important that whites learn to love Negroes, he considered it a more urgent task that they stop lynching them. Since the days of civil rights, movements have become a part of the political landscape. A mixed blessing they may well be, but their fundamental premise is unassailable. If women and other minorities are to achieve equal rights, if the earth is to be preserved from needless ravage and destruction, concerted action is necessary. "Thought, by itself," the great theoretician remarked, "moves nothing" (1139a36–37).

Given that doing the right thing requires practice in virtue, we can now expound a bit on that specific virtue that guides practice, Aristotelian *phronesis*. If you would allow me a little liberty with the text, I would define practical wisdom as follows: At the right time

and place, the right person acts in the right way for the right purpose.[5] To know what that means, Aristotle, ever the practical
thinker, urges us to look at the practically wise person and how she
acts. For that reason our thoughts have been tracing Rosa Parks's
action.

"Right Time and Place"

Nowhere is the very real and sometimes frightening contingency of
human acts more apparent than in considerations of time and place.
Human action is always inserted at a particular time and in a particular place, so, like Heraclitus's river, you can never step into the
same act in exactly the same way and expect the same effect. To
gauge the right time and the right place for an act, then, is probably
the most difficult skill an actor can acquire. Like any other skill, the
ability to act in the appropriate place and in a timely fashion is partly
a gift, partly the fruit of imagination, virtue, and learned experience.
It also depends on the goddess the Romans addressed as "Fortuna"
and gamblers invoke as "Lady Luck." We are all in the position of
"Monday morning quarterbacks" who find it easier to assess acts in
hindsight than to divine them in foresight. Prohibition was enacted
at the wrong time and place: that is the almost universal consensus
now, but not so in 1920. Sometimes tax cuts work; sometimes they
don't. And sometimes the examination of entrails seems about as
reliable as the prognostications of economists. Politics is an uncertain and even a risky business.

Although acts like Rosa Parks's can seem to come out of
nowhere, almost miraculously, they can never be purely a *creatio ex
nihilo* (creation out of nothing). Time and place are givens; actors do
not create them. But there is a sense in which they can be chosen:
we can choose now rather than later, here rather than there. A sense
of timing is important and Rosa Parks certainly had it. In 1953, the
Negroes in Baton Rouge, Louisiana, had successfully integrated the
buses by means of a boycott. Their efforts, spearheaded by T. J.
Jemison, had been well publicized through the informal network of
Negro churches in the deep South. A year later, in 1954, the
Supreme Court, in *Brown v. the Board of Education in Topeka, Kansas*,

outlawed segregation in the public schools and signaled the death knell for any continuing legal support for the invidious Jim Crow practices in the southern states. As for "the right place": Montgomery, Alabama, though a bastion of the old south, was ripe for a challenge to the system of segregation. Negro frustration with the bus situation had reached a boiling point. In the months prior to Rosa Parks's civil disobedience, several Negroes had been arrested for refusing to obey the segregation ordinance on the buses. Mrs. Parks herself, as we have already mentioned, had confronted bus drivers about the seating policy. Though the Negro community was riddled with a "crippling factionalism," some of those divergent groups were poised for action.[6] Rosa Parks had been secretary and now was a youth group leader in an independent and feisty branch of the NAACP, headed by E. D. Nixon. A Woman's Political Council, organized at Alabama State College under the leadership of Mary Fair Burks and Jo Ann Robinson, had created a powerful network of women who would become responsible for the initial impetus and continued success of the boycott. Finally, a new, dynamic young minister had ·recently accepted the pastorate at Dexter Avenue Baptist Church, Dr. Martin Luther King, Jr. The time and place were indeed right for a challenge to a system that undeniably oppressed Montgomery's fifty thousand Negroes, who constituted 39 percent of the city's population. One might speculate that had not Rosa Parks ignited the spark, someone else surely would have. But such a hypothetical speculation is beside the point. It was Rosa Parks who possessed the imagination and courage to seize the moment. It was *her* act.

One of the most important things to be learned from *her* act, however, is the utter uniqueness of great human acts. Because it was done at a specific time and place and done so well, it does inspire emulation but it cannot be repeated. That is why there can be no handbooks or manuals for public action. There is no substitute for a political actor's practical wisdom which enables her to discern the right time and place. Robert Sokolowski says that manuals create "false copies of prudence" that too often destroy the goods they are trying to promote by "not letting practical intelligence deliberate and choose on the scene."[7] The good that is to be done must be discerned within the situation, not apart from it; to do this, a good deal of moral imagination must be brought to bear in the rush of events. Such practical imagination and intelligence is what civil rights leaders would exhibit time and again during those early years of the struggle.

The decision to boycott the buses in Montgomery, following Mrs. Parks's arrest, is a good case in point. Later, mass civil disobedience was used very effectively by Negroes throughout the South. There in Montgomery, at that time, mass arrests would certainly have been premature and likely disastrous. Because it did not require breaking the law, the boycott could mobilize large numbers of Negroes in a way that allowed them to express their anger and persuade the bus company to change its policies. It too was a brilliant exercise of Aristotelian *phronesis*.

Even so, neither Rosa Parks nor Martin Luther King, nor any of the Montgomery leaders, could have predicted the incredible effect her act would have upon the city of Montgomery and the course of U.S. history. She could hardly have guessed how her little act of protest would mobilize the faction-ridden Negro community, spark the unprecedented year-long boycott that would end bus desegregation in the South, and ignite the civil rights movement under the auspices of the Southern Christian Leadership Conference. But that is the nature of great public deeds, which can create what Hannah Arendt called a boundless "web of interaction" whose influences are impossible to predict.[8] A striking example of the boundless and unpredictable character of human action can be found in a story Taylor Branch tells in his superlative chronicle of the civil rights movement, *Parting the Waters*:

> A few days after the Holt Street mass meeting [where Martin L. King announced the boycott] one of the teachers at a Methodist missionary school near Nagpur, India, rushed outside to investigate a bellowing noise that had pierced the early morning stillness. In the hut next door, he found his colleague James Lawson still in a fit of shouting and clapping and foot-stomping. Such joyous abandon was almost as alarming to the teacher as the violence he had feared, because he knew Lawson as the essence of the cerebral personality—a man

who had worn spectacles since the age of four, whose superior manner and precise articulation smothered any hint of emotionalism in his character. Yet now, even after Theopolis burst through the door, Lawson was still dancing, and could only point to a story in the English edition of the Nagpur *Times* about how thousands of Negroes were refusing to ride segregated buses in a small American city. (p. 143)

Branch points out the marvelous irony of the story: Here a young man had traveled halfway around the globe to the origin of the Gandhian spirit only to find it moribund. While back in the States, only a few hundred miles from James Lawson's home, the true spirit of Gandhi was breaking forth. Lawson would soon return home and join King as one of the chief architects of the civil rights movement. So, in a sort of human Gaia effect, the small act of a Montgomery seamstress flew on the butterfly wings of the media and sparked a tornado of rejoicing in Nagpur, India.

So boundless, so unpredictable, so wonderfully unique are the great deeds of actors that their meaning can only be captured in a story. However needful political scientists and even philosophers are to the public realm, it is finally the storyteller, like the blind Homer, who comes upon the scene after the act is done and preserves it in memory for later generations. While it may seem that the human story is a never-ending one, the storyteller can bring a certain kind of closure to the particular stories within human history. In the "once upon a time in a land far away" we are presented with the universal element in all stories, namely that the deeds told about happened in a particular time and place and, for that very reason, cannot be repeated. And yet, in the final irony, it is these stories about deeds done that can be repeated, can be continually retold, and thus ensure that the acts and actors continue to live in the moral imagination of those who come after.

"Right Person"

However difficult it is to gauge the right time and place for a political act, no one questioned even then that Rosa Parks was the "right person." On Monday night, the first day of the bus boycott, at a mass rally at the Holt Street Baptist Church, Martin Luther King characterized her in those rhetorical tones that would become so familiar in the ensuing years: "Nobody can doubt the boundless outreach of her integrity. Nobody can doubt the height of her character. Nobody can doubt the depths of her Christian commitment."[9] In a sea of uncertain events, it is a person's character that is the only sure ballast. Still, one might wonder why a victim's character should be so important or even relevant in the face of obvious injustice. The answer to that question will tell us something about how character gets embedded in our acts and just how intricate the task of practical wisdom can be. A thinker, not necessarily a wise one, who was willing to make an ethical assessment of the Jim Crow practices in the South could, without too much trouble, judge them immoral. But when that thinker wishes to become an actor and must decide what to do in the face of this evil, the matter becomes a good deal more complicated. A glance back at the situation in Montgomery in 1955 should reveal just that.

It is now well known that the Negro leadership in Montgomery were seeking to test in court the ordinances that segregated the buses. Two opportunities arose in March and October that same year when two Negro women were arrested for refusing to give up their seats. Their cases were not pursued, in part because E. D. Nixon and others judged that they were not the right persons. (One young woman was an unwed, pregnant teenager who had used abusive language during the confrontation; the other woman lived in a clapboard shack with her alcoholic father.) Some argued that the character of the defendants was irrelevant and, strictly speaking, they were right. The blindfolded goddess who holds the scale of justice cannot see whether or not the litigant is pregnant or where she lives. But the political issue required at this time and place a stricter standard. The litigant most likely would have to endure a long series of appeals, lots of publicity, and a great deal of hatred. It was not only important that she have the courage to withstand her upcoming ordeal, it was equally important that she be a fitting representation to the public of the dignified but firm resistance of Negroes to segregation. In addition, the leadership did not want any distraction from the issue at hand; they did not want to give opponents (or even sympathizers) an excuse to focus on some other tangential point. Stereotypes of Negroes were rampant at this time (lazy, shiftless, happy-go-lucky, watermelon-eating folks), and it was important to break once and for all those false images. The issue was not simply an abstract affirmation of a legal right; what was at stake was a good deal more, a delicate and difficult negotiation over a people's place in the community. E. D. Nixon knew this and he was right, I think, to require the "character test."

There was little doubt that Rosa Parks could pass the strictest of character tests. As future events would bear out, she would become more than just a litigant but the veritable icon of the civil rights movement. Television cameras and newspaper photographs captured the quiet, dignified, unruffled demeanor of this petite Negro with the wire-rimmed glasses and plaited hair. In the midst of the turmoil of events she was a fixed, serene point, a moral touchstone for anyone willing to ask what must be done. I can hardly imagine another example of where a political symbol better expressed the deepest reality of a movement's moral core. In his *Rhetoric*, Aristotle remarked that the character of the speaker is "the most powerful means of persuasion."[10] Clearly, Rosa Parks's character persuaded many who saw or heard her through the media. If this proper, dignified, church-going lady was willing to endure the humiliation of arrest to protest an injustice, how could she be ignored? In a way that no "rabble-rouser" could, she spoke to the conscience of America.

In the media today there is a good deal of talk, most of it beside the point, about the character of public officials. At a time when "image is everything," it is more important (as Machiavelli might have put it) that a public official appear to have character than that he or she actually possess it. The politician must avoid, at all cost, the *image* of moral weakness. (The "wimp factor" in George Bush's presidency is but one of numerous examples that could be cited here.) However useful the *appearance* of being courageous, just, and beneficent might be in getting elected or in maintaining one's stature in the polls, Machiavelli (and I suppose some campaign managers today) would worry that such character traits might actually impede the process of acquiring and maintaining power. For all its realpolitik, those who proffer such a view, however, fail to notice (a character flaw, perhaps) one important reality: the possibilities for acting that are disclosed only to someone who possesses a good character.

Because she was already a just person, Rosa Parks could seize an opportunity to act justly that others might miss. Robert Sokolowski speaks of a moral blindness that can occur not as a result of failing to see the facts but as a result of lacking the ability to appraise a situation properly.[11] This "aspect-blindness" (the phrase is Wittgenstein's) can result from a defect in character. Certainly on that fateful day in Montgomery, neither the bus driver nor the white riders could see or appreciate the deeper moral issue. Even the Negroes who moved to the back of the bus, perhaps because they did not want to be hassled, missed something that Rosa Parks did not. Her appraisal of the situation and the way she acted emerged from a character already disposed to act courageously and justly. Her act breathed new moral life into a situation where others saw only the status quo.

Character provides, finally, a nice polarity to the boundless unpredictability of action. Because character is dispositional, we can anticipate a person's acts; we can rely, for example, on a good politician's honesty or even be wary of a bad character's promise to deliver the goods. Unlike the predictions of some behavioral scientists that factor out individual freedom, a person's character can offer us a measure of reliability in the realm of human affairs without denigrating choice and initiative. We cannot always predict what a person will do or the way she will do it, but we can expect a just person to act justly—and that is what Rosa Parks did.

There is much more that needs to be said about character in public life than this little coda can supply. But the example of Rosa Parks's act demonstrates the old scholastic axiom *actio sequitur esse* (action follows being). That would be, I think, the right place to start.

"Right Purpose"

My friendly tennis competitor loves to discount my good shots (what few they are) with the old retort: "Even a blind squirrel will occasionally find a nut." It is of course possible to hit a good shot (or even to do the right thing) without seeing why. "Dumb luck," we sometimes say of our stumbling upon the right shot—or the right answer. Beasts were often called "dumb" because they could not speak, could not render an account of their acts. What distinguishes their behavior (undeniably better than ours at times) from our acts is the fact that we explain, justify, and even excuse ourselves. We can unwittingly do what is right, but if our acts are to be specifically human we need to offer reasons for what we do. The reason for that is the fact (explained in detail in chapter 2) that our acts embody purposes, and if the meanings of our acts are to be laid open, those purposes must be distilled out. It is not enough for humans simply to hit the mark; they must know why they hit it, if for no other reason than that to hit it consistently requires that we know what we are doing.

It is more appropriate to speak of "right purpose" than the more standard "right reason" because, as Aristotle notes, practical wisdom embodies both "right reason" *and* "right desire."[12] We are all too familiar with the situation where right reason is needed to check a faulty desire—the Black Forest chocolate cake I so desperately want is, I know, not good for me. But it can also happen that right desires can correct a flawed reason—as we saw in chapter 3 with Tocqueville's farmer whose charitable deed failed to be captured by his self-interested explanation.

It is hardly difficult to distill out of Rosa Parks's act her purpose. What she wanted was to be treated fairly—not just for herself but for her race. Those who knew her knew that she was not out for any sort of fame or recognition or even martyrdom. What was on her mind and in her heart was justice, pure and simple. Justice was the principle embodied in her act at its source and as its goal. One could not render any meaningful account of her deed without explaining it in those moral terms.

The whole significance of the civil rights movement rested on its claim that its inspiration and goal was a moral (and religious) one. Martin Luther King was acutely sensitive to this dimension. He continually worried about the moral issue of means and ends and in his own retelling of the Montgomery events worried that acts like Rosa Parks's and the subsequent boycott could be "used to unethical and unchristian ends."[13] He was well aware that the *way* he had chosen needed to be grounded in moral purposes if he was to distinguish the movement's tactics from those of the segregationists who employed similar methods (boycotts, for example). "Our purposes," he argued, "were altogether different" because they aimed at giving "birth to justice and freedom."[14] Then in a carefully laid out argument that drew on the traditional doctrine of double effect, he argued that the intentions of the movement were not to hurt white businesses, not to put them "out of business but to put justice in business."[15] He indicated, further, that he stopped using the word "boycott" and adopted the Thoreau phrase "noncooperation with evil" not as a linguistic ploy but in an effort to clearly distinguish his purposes from those of segregationists.[16]

One could argue that it was the moral capital built up by such language that made the civil rights movement so tremendously effective. When the movement lost its moorings in that moral language and in the churches that nurtured it, it collapsed into power grabs by ideological factions. Writing recently about contemporary politics, the astute reporter E. J. Dionne remarked of the civil rights movement: "The most pragmatic course was the moral course."[17] That bit of wisdom, he ruefully concludes, is just what is absent in today's political struggles. We will return to this issue later; for now I want to continue my reflection on the practical wisdom of Rosa Parks's great act.

"Right Way"

Nowhere is Rosa Parks's character and purpose more in evidence than in the *way* she performed her act. Granted, sitting in a bus and refusing to move hardly seems that complicated a task, however frightening it might have been to try it in 1955 in Montgomery, Alabama. Yet Mrs. Parks's demeanor, more than anything else, was responsible for this act becoming so historically significant. To understand that, we need to mention how diabolically clever southern authorities could be in thwarting efforts to overturn segregationist statutes. In the case of the rambunctious teenager I mentioned earlier, the Montgomery judge convicted her of the charge of assault, based on the preposterous "evidence" of her verbal abuse. Then he shrewdly levied only a minimal fine, ensuring that she would not be viewed as a martyr. Finally, he dismissed the charge of violating the segregation ordinance, preempting any further challenge in the courts. Had Mrs. Parks's demeanor, then, been anything other than it was—respectful and dignified—she could have been charged with assault or disorderly conduct, and once again a potential legal challenge to segregated buses would have been forestalled. As it was, the authorities had but two options—either release her and thus admit the unenforceability of the segregation laws, or charge her with the only possible violation, refusing to obey the bus ordinance. The authorities chose the latter course, convicting and fining her and thus opening the way for the legal appeal that would lead almost a year later to the Supreme Court's ruling that outlawed Alabama's segregated bus system. This deeply religious woman certainly knew there was no inherent contradiction between being as gentle as a dove and as wise as a serpent.

Deeds are often judged on the basis of their efficacy: that is, did they accomplish what they set out to do? By that standard, Rosa Parks's refusal to obey the busing ordinance achieved its most explicit purpose—the desegregation of Montgomery's buses. Great deeds, however, are more than just a question of tactics, however brilliantly executed. It is not Rosa Parks's cleverness that evokes our admiration, but something grander—dare we say—noble. The serene, courageous dignity with which Rosa Parks endured the danger and humiliation of arrest leaves us in awe. In the Greek sense of the noble, the *aristos*, her singular act exploited the situation of injustice in the best possible way. Could we imagine doing it any better?

Something there is, in the democratic temper, that doesn't love a hero (to echo Robert Frost's "Mending Wall"). Perhaps the noble deed is too painful a reminder of our conceit of equality; at any rate, it often inspires in us nothing more than green-eyed envy. But what such envy masks, of course, is our own weakness. In this age when self-esteem has achieved a cultlike status, it is easy to forget that before a noble act can inspire emulation it should provoke a healthy shame. And that is what Rosa Parks's example did. Her arrest shamed the various factions in the Negro community enough that they put aside their petty squabbles in favor of concerted action; it shamed the large number of Negroes who hated the Jim Crow practices but were too fearful to do anything about them; and, finally, it shamed some of Montgomery's whites to urge a change in what they knew were immoral practices. So it no longer mattered whether you had a little money or were dirt poor, whether you went to Holt Street Baptist or Trinity Lutheran or whether your allegiance was with the NAACP or the Women's Political Council or, finally, whether you were black or white—all that mattered was that Rosa Parks had refused to "make it light" on herself and now provided a soaring inspiration to anyone willing to take up the burden of correcting injustice.

Noble deeds, however, can be so forbidding that even those capable of being inspired by them are loath to follow the example they set. The aristocratic conceit is that only the few are capable of such heroism. At the end of *A Tale of Two Cities*, which records the end of aristocracy in Paris, Sydney Carton's noble martyrdom goes unnoticed by the mob, and, had they known, their response would hardly have been an admiring one. By contrast, Rosa Parks's act was able to invite others into the orbit of its influence and spark a response. It was at one and the same time noble *and* democratic. It is this invitational quality of her act that is responsible—more than anything else, I think—for the genius of her deed. Public deeds are by their very nature performed in the presence of others. Their efficacy depends on the impact they have on others. Noble, democratic deeds invite others into the actor's world and create possibilities for acting that were not there beforehand. Merely imitating her act by getting arrested on the buses (as I already noted) would have been unwise. Staying *off* the buses, however, brilliantly emulated the example set by Mrs. Parks in a way that allowed for maximum participation. Refusing to ride the bus was, after all, an incredibly simple gesture. Everyone could and did do it. Making the boycott work, of course, was a tremendously complex task that demanded sophisticated organization and at times real sacrifices. But for over a year the boycott continued with the nearly unanimous support of the Negro community in Montgomery.

"History," Hannah Arendt remarks, "is full of examples of the impotence of the strong and superior man who does not know how to enlist the help, the co-acting of his fellow men."[18] In Montgomery, Alabama, it was a humble, nonviolent woman who almost effortlessly invited her fellow citizens to demonstrate the power of concerted, democratic action.

If we remain focused on public acts and the way they are performed, it may be possible to avoid the pitfalls into which disputants about nonviolence often seem to fall.[19] Later on in the civil rights movement, the question whether nonviolence must be accepted as a total way of life or simply adopted as one tactic among others was hotly debated. Put that way, the question is dangerously abstract and needlessly divisive. The opponents of nonviolence invariably point out that the requirement to act nonviolently always and without exception is an unrealistic and excessive moral demand. But to accept nonviolence merely as a tactic belittles the act and denigrates the moral commitment of those early civil rights heroes. An act like Rosa Parks's, however, was neither purely instrumental nor rigidly ideological; it was (as I have tried to argue) the best way to do it. It may be important to ask whether nonviolence is the only way to act whenever and wherever we act. But the danger in raising that question in such an a priori way is that we narrow the range within which practical wisdom can operate: that is, we fail to consider how this act, done nonviolently, may be the best way to act at this particular time, in this particular place. Such a consideration opens up the act to be evaluated and admired by pacifist and nonpacifist alike.

Here we can note how nonviolence fosters that inclusivity that was characterized earlier as the hallmark of a great deed. Even one's opponents are engaged in a way that requires argument, thus inhibiting, at least somewhat, the outbreak of violence.

Civic disturbances like the one in Los Angeles in the spring of 1992 are, by contrast, incredibly divisive. A youth throwing a rock through a window may be making an invitation to loot because if people join him there will be less chance of being caught. But if too many join, the spoils will be greatly diminished in what ultimately is a self-serving act. Rosa Parks certainly wanted justice for herself but, as Aristotle remarks, the practically wise citizens are those who "can discern the things that are good for themselves and for human beings": that is, both the individual's *and* the common good.[20]

One need not be a pacifist, then, to affirm a significant moral difference between violence and nonviolence. Violent acts have an instrumental character; they are justified by the appropriateness of their ends and the efficacy with which their goals are achieved. A person who defends herself against a rapist justifies whatever violence she uses by an appeal to her own safety against an unjust attacker and by a calculation, however quickly made, that the means she employs may be successful. Nonviolent acts, too, can be instrumental, but they can also be performed, as acts of friendship are, for their own sake, as ends in themselves. Because they are so common, so everyday, so familiar, we tend to forget that these nonviolent acts form the warp and woof of our public, and private, lives. Where violence becomes the modus operandi, as in a reign of terror, we are quickly reminded of how precious, even extraordinary, is our taken-for-granted public world where nonviolence is the standard. If nonviolence is the appropriate form of public life, that does not mean, of course, that every nonviolent act is wise or good. It does mean, though, that every public act, so long as it is nonviolent, can become part of the rhetoric of persuasion—argument, debate, voting, civil disobedience even—upon which a healthy polity thrives.

The great danger today, no less than in the sixties, is that violence and nonviolence are viewed merely as different strategies on a progressive continuum of public options. Some factions of the pro-life movement, for example, unlike the early civil rights movement, have not displayed a collective conscience that is sensitive to the crucial moral distinction between public acts of civil disobedience and private harassment of, and even violence against, clinic workers. Those of us who believe that abortion is the unjustified taking of innocent human life cannot but be horrified by the fate of the unborn in abortion clinics. But I wonder how many in the movement are aware of the fateful line that is crossed when legitimate public protest and civil disobedience are confused with vandalism and bombings. These latter acts express a profound political (and perhaps even religious) despair and, unwittingly or not, are equivalent to a declaration of civil war. It is not easy to attribute a reason for this fateful flaw. It may, in part, be due to the fact that so many in the pro-life movement have so little political experience. (Remember Aristotle's preference for the person of experience over the person of mere conviction.) The failure may also partly be due to the fact that the standard formula remains: "Is nonviolence a tactic or way of life?" Since so many in the movement are not pacifists, the only feasible alternative seems to be the adoption of nonviolence as a strategic option. Whatever the cause—and one can never discount lack of virtue either—the movement would do better if it remains faithful to that example it claims to honor—the civil rights movement. The pro-life movement may want more people like Randall Terry; what it needs, though, is another Rosa Parks.

A New Beginning

"At the right time and place, the right person acts for the right reason and in the right way." By following Aristotle's lead and by looking closely at one public act, I hope I have been able to shed some light on some of the basic features of public action. Like a great text, however, a deed like Rosa Parks's offers an inexhaustible richness for anyone who would pay close attention to it. There is, then, one other dimension to the events in Montgomery in 1955 that bears mentioning. For many who witnessed those events, and even for some who just learned about them in the media, those deeds sparked a startled wonder in the face of something unpredictable and quite new. It was as though a new page in history had been turned, and even for those in whom these same events generated more horror than wonder, there probably was the sense that something frighteningly new was happening, something that the participants could at that time scarcely comprehend. But even now, four decades later, the events in that winter of 1955 and 1956 seem wondrous to behold and perhaps even a bit frightening insofar as such an awesome power was unleashed into the body politic, a power capable of transforming and, if we are honest about it, devastating a polity. While this dimension of newness takes us beyond the Aristotelian definition of *phronesis*, hints of it can already be found in the respect, even reverence, the Greeks held for the great deed. While the Greek view of history may have been cyclic and does not seem to allow for the irruption of the new into it, the practically wise agent of Aristotle must, perforce, bring out new possibilities in action that were but dimly perceived before. Rosa Parks's act sets an example, and something more: it initiates something altogether new. Here again we are face-to-face with our humanity and its utmost possibilities. Hannah Arendt frequently quoted a line in Augustine, a thought that expresses the unique possibilities that each new birth brings into the human community: "So that there might be a beginning, a human being was created."[21] Each human actor as a unique newcomer in human affairs is capable of setting a new precedent. That is why a community both welcomes and is a bit fearful of the newcomers, whether they be youths from within or strangers from without. However disrupting the newcomers can be, the oldtimers know that without "new blood" the community will stagnate and die. For the most part, however, and not without good reason, our everyday, routine acts barely hint at the possibilities of uniqueness. But every once in a while a Rosa Parks comes along and initiates something miraculous into the public arena.

In human affairs, unlike the divine *creatio ex nihilo*, there are no absolutely new beginnings. (Arendt thought revolutions came closest.) Every new example is conditioned by what has gone before, and Rosa Parks's act was no exception. Indeed, history is not without examples of heroic acts of resistance. Socrates' refusal to follow the Thirty Tyrants' order to arrest and execute illegally the general, Leon of Salamis, is one such case; Thomas More's refusal to sign the Oath of Supremacy, another; and Thoreau's well-known night in jail for refusing to pay taxes to support the Mexican-American war, still another. But each of these cases, as Hannah Arendt points out in her astute article on "Civil Disobedience," are individual acts of private conscience that exist only on the periphery of the political.[22] Tellingly, Socrates reports that when ordered to carry out the unjust dictate, he, quite simply, "went home." More took great pains to ensure his silence was not construed in any political sense, and Thoreau's distaste for politics is well known. In these examples there is no concerted attempt to engage others in a political movement. The heroic resistance of the people of Le Chambon comes closest to the Montgomery example, but, even here, what was done had to be done in secret.[23] Rosa Parks's civil disobedience and the subsequent boycott set a new American paradigm for political action. Gandhi had already demonstrated the tremendous power of noncooperation in India, but the civil rights movement from its inception was very much American, very democratic in the way Tocqueville described the American penchant for civic organizing. At this time, all over the South, what Aldon Morris has called "local movement centers" had begun to spring up almost spontaneously.[24] A good while before the Southern Christian Leadership Conference would give the movement coordination and direction, church-based centers of political action had formed in Baton Rouge, Tallahassee, Albany, Birmingham, and elsewhere.

Prior to this upsurge in political action, Negroes had but few options in the face of segregation: the morally enervating route of reluctant acquiescence, the quixotic path of violence, or the laborious and lengthy legal challenges. The latter, urged chiefly by the NAACP, had been successful in eliminating legalized segregation; but besides proceeding at a snail's pace, legal suits by their very nature could involve only a handful of highly trained professionals. Though it would demand courage and endurance, refusing to sit in the back of the bus required no special license. Here was a way for the common citizen to act that eschewed violence and yet could be powerfully effective. Here was a possibility, unformed in the moral imagination of Socrates, More, and Thoreau, that allowed for a public civic dissent that aimed at persuading others to change for the sake of a public good.

Here, finally, was one of politics' "superb surprises" (to borrow a phrase from Emily Dickinson). Arising as it did out of the somnolent fifties, this new paradigm of political action certainly confounded the prognostications of the best political scientists. When all is said and done, there remains in the nature of events the capacity to surprise and astound us. The rapid disintegration of communism, the people's revolution in the Philippines, the meteoric rise of a Vaclav Havel all attest to the wondrous freshness that politics at least sometimes demonstrates. Of course, not all surprises are superb, and so we witness with horror the renewal of ethnic hatreds in Europe, the unforeseen rise (and fall) of a David Duke, the unexpected verdict in the Rodney King trial. Such is the difficult but human wager of politics. But when it comes in the face of the more mundane but entrenched feeling of many Americans that public action is fruitless and ineffective, it is good to remember that every so often an ordinary citizen like Rosa Parks, who is willing to shoulder the burden of the public good, can make a difference.

Solon and Political Action Today

Given the greatness of its origin and its astonishing success in those early years, it is not at all surprising that the civil rights movement became a powerful model for political action; and, even today, four decades after it began, it continues to inspire civic-minded activists. Unfortunately, for some who would act in the public arena, protest movements have provided the only paradigm for public action. Extending the protest movement model to every aspect of public life, however, raises two profound difficulties. First of all, the flexibility that practical wisdom must have as it deliberates on the scene is severely limited if not outright jeopardized. The events of Montgomery cannot serve as an instructional manual to be scrupulously followed each and every time a public debate occurs.[25] Second, if protest becomes the modus operandi of politics, then, consciously or not, the legitimacy of the democratic regime is called into question. This is not the place to contest directly the claim that our constitutional polity has lost its legitimacy. Rather, I would call attention to the fact that the original notion of civil dissent to a specific policy always assumed a prior assent to a constitutional order that was viewed as capable of correcting the challenged injustice.[26] The great power of acts like Rosa Parks's rests in their ability to appeal to that order and to the overwhelming number of citizens who likewise assent to it. To dissent always and everywhere can be politically disastrous because it creates, often enough, a self-righteous marginalized elite that is incapable of appealing to the moral and political commitments of the citizenry. Rosa Parks's act, by contrast, can serve as a paradigm of political action because its meaning transcends the adamantine logic of some protest movements. Still, the form that her act took was civil disobedience; what is needed, then, is to demonstrate how the spirit of that act might be transferred, through the agency of practical wisdom, into the less dramatic but more common events that constitute our civic life.

A small example might be illustrative. In my little city there has been an ongoing discussion about the best way to structure representation on the city council. Should representatives be chosen exclusively from districts, exclusively at large, or by some combination of the two? Obviously, there is an important moral principle at stake: namely, fairness in representation. But doing the right thing involves so much more and demands a practical wisdom that is in touch with the history, character, and diversity of the city and its neighborhoods. Any decision must involve the public—Rosa Parks's example is still authoritative here—but beyond that, the politics of protest offers little guidance and would even be imprudent. What is needed is a practical imagination that can seize on the right solution and develop a consensus about it.

I want, then, to conclude this chapter with some discussion of more contemporary political issues in a way that also extends the notion of public action developed thus far. We need a new guide for that, and fortunately one is at hand—though, as another long-dead white European male, he may need a little dusting off! I'd like to employ, then, one of the "Seven Wise Men" of the ancient traditions and its greatest statesman: Solon.[27]

In recent years there has been a great deal of discussion about what is called "the political center." Politicians need it defined so that they can tap into the huge reservoir of votes it presumably holds. To define oneself or be defined by one's opponent as outside that center can mean almost certain defeat, as Democratic presidential candidates in the 1980s discovered. There is, of course, nothing intrinsically good about the center nor evil about being outside it: Rosa Parks's act would have to be put, at the very least, on the periphery of the political center. Jesse Jackson reminded Democrats in 1992 that the political center is not to be confused with the moral center. Still, insofar as the center can represent the majority or even the consensus view of things, it is a concept well worth exploring and a topic about which Solon offers, I believe, a bit of timely wisdom.

Talk today of the political center brings to mind the ancient Greek ideal of the middle way (*to meson*). However, for the Greeks, the middle way, as a centrist principle, had nothing to do with the tyranny of the majority; it did not even mean, for those *aristoi* who espoused it, majority rule. Nor did it connote the safest, least controversial, or mediocre way of acting. Rather, the middle way meant the act that threaded its way between the extremes of excess and deficiency: the act that hit the target and thus could be described in no other terms than "excellent," "the best," or "just right." A few examples from Solon's efforts to strike a middle path will offer an illustrative contrast with today's political pandering to that ill-defined center.

Perhaps Solon's greatest accomplishment as a statesman was his ability to hold in check the disruptive force of Athenian factions while not giving in to the temptation of tyranny. Despite the fact that tyranny was familiar to the Greeks, during Solon's public life there was little inclination to establish one in Athens, particularly since Solon was the only likely candidate and he assiduously resisted it. "Tyranny provides a lofty vantage point; only there's no way down," he quipped.[28] His attention, then, was turned to the mediation of the various factional disputes within the city walls. The American experience also has been free of tyranny, though for somewhat different reasons. True, George Washington seems to have been as little inclined to tyrannical rule as Solon, but the American experience and the temper of individualism create a particularly inhospitable soil for one-man rule. Factionalism, on the other hand, has been a continuing thorn in the side of our body politic; it seems to be an inherent and continuing trial in the course of any democratic regime. The issue is, how do we strike a balance between the plurality which alone can provide a richness to a polity and the unity of purpose without which a community cannot long endure? The current discussion of diversity is an obvious case in point. The old "melting pot" analogy is criticized as too oppressive in its effacement of difference while the "tossed salad" substitution seems coolly indifferent to unity. Where is Goldilocks's "just right" porridge when we need it! Actually, none of these gastronomical metaphors are all that illuminating since they leave unexplained the nature of the unity and diversity in a civic community. Barbara Jordan was on the right track when she told the 1992 Democratic National Convention that the hallowed phrase *e pluribus unum* best captures the meaning of the American experiment, though it is the task of each generation to articulate anew just how that diverse unity and unified diversity works.

For the American experiment, James Madison's *Federalist Papers* No. 10 is the benchmark text. He was well acquainted with Solon and the Athenian *polis* and felt that the new order brought out by the American polity had one distinct advantage over democratic Athens—a system of representative government. Just as the separation of powers provided a powerful check against tyranny, so representative government, as opposed to pure democracy, checked the dangerous effects of factionalism. What is particularly heinous about factionalism (as both Madison and Solon saw it) is that insofar as factions represent particular interests, they are capable of rending apart the common good. Given that human beings are not angels (a well-known sentiment of Madison's), it is not possible to extirpate private interests. Thus factions, rooted as they are in our nature as humans, will always be with us, so long as a government is committed to the idea of individual liberty. Madison thought it best to try to moderate the effects of factional strife by creating a representative system that mediated between the passionate interests of groups and the decision makers. Representatives, Madison hoped, would tend to be more dispassionate and, coming from extensive geographical areas, would likely diminish the local passions of particular interest groups: ". . . the public voice, pronounced by the representatives of the people, will be more consonant to the public good. . . ."[29] There is undoubted wisdom in this account of republican government that explains the political purpose of representation in terms other than sheer numbers. There are problems with it also. Time and technology have succeeded in effacing somewhat the distance between citizens and their representatives that Madison thought so necessary. Factions can have an immediate impact today via the electronic media. Also, paid lobbyists and special interest groups that have ensconced themselves permanently in local, state, and national legislatures have created an impact unforeseen by the federalist authors. Furthermore, a significant criticism of Madison's analysis has been to question why he discounts the obvious ameliorative effects of moral and religious constraints on the two sources of faction, private greed and personal gain. If our drive for personal gain always trumps moral and religious strictures, as Madison seems to think, why would anyone assume representatives would be any more inclined to act on behalf of the public good than their electors? Madison's tough "realism" about the self-interested motives of human beings is, as J. Budziszewski points out, not all that realistic.[30] Indeed representative government can work only if a sufficient number of citizens take the public good seriously. Republics flourish where there are citizens devoted to the public good, not individuals subject to their own or someone else's will. As the turmoil that succeeded the breakup of communism in Eastern Europe demonstrated, there are no shortcuts to the path of civic virtue.

Despite these caveats, it is worthwhile noting how strenuously Madison is seeking here a middle way. For him, representative government is a mean between a chaotic, unworkable "pure democracy" and a monarchy. Unlike Madison, however, Solon believed that civic virtue could be an effective check on factional violence. Greed, self-indulgence, injustice: these vices for Solon were the seedbed of factionalism. So, in tempering the two most obdurate factions in his day, the landed wealthy and the propertyless poor, he sought to check the greed of the former and the envy of the latter. He demonstrated what today might be called a "preferential option for the poor" because he saw them as the most vulnerable and defenseless group in the city. His throwing off the burden of debt (the *seisacheia*) the poor had accumulated, temporarily infuriated the wealthier citizens, but, as Plutarch notes, they eventually realized that his policy served their long-term interest by creating a more stable community.[31] By refusing to institute a drastic land redistribution policy and by requiring work of those who were assisted by government, Solon risked the anger of the lower classes but ensured in the long run a more responsible and diligent citizenry. He perceived the enervating effects of the dole long before the Republicans "discovered" it in 1980. His efforts at cutting a "middle way" are captured in his own somewhat melodramatic verse:

> To the common people (*Demo*) I gave so much power as is sufficient; neither robbing them of dignity (*times*) nor giving them too much; And those who had power and were marvelously rich, even for these I contrived that they suffered no harm. I stood with a mighty shield in front of both classes and suffered neither of them to prevail unjustly.[32]

Now Solon's middle way is certainly a centrist position, but it is a far cry from the secure, vote-rich center that American politicians seem to lust after. The metaphors he uses to describe the vulnerability of his middle way are starkly revelatory: he pictures himself on one occasion as a wolf circling around to keep a pack of hounds at bay; in another poem he is an outpost exposed between two opposing battle lines. The real political center is no easier a place to stand than the moral center.

Those rather violent metaphors, though, are in danger of overstating the case because, for Solon to have been as successful as he was, he had to be able to build a consensus among the Athenians. He was a statesman who possessed considerable powers of persuasion and was called "wise" not without reason. When asked whether he had given the Athenians the best possible laws, this "great lawgiver," as he was called, replied: "The best they could receive."[33] He knew that the authority of law best rested not on arms (as Hobbes later would have it) but in the willingness of citizens to obey. And that willingness rested, as he said, on citizens being persuaded that "the practice of justice was more advantageous than the breaking of the law." There is a great deal of practical wisdom or what Solon called "a prepared mind" (*noos artios*) on display here, particularly in his ability to decipher what was the best thing for Athens at that time.[34]

That such practical wisdom is not to be equated with a timid prudence is best demonstrated by one of Solon's laws that Plutarch describes as peculiar and paradoxical. Though he fought factions all his life, he enacted a law which required citizens, under pain of disenfranchisement, to take sides in factional disputes. Aristotle, though, saw what Solon was doing. Commenting on that law, he noted the tendency of certain citizens "out of sheer indifference, to let things slide."[35] Aristotle's chilling word for an event that unfolds without the intervention of responsible citizens is *automaton.*[36] I can think of no more frightening but accurate description of the apathetic citizen. By contrast, it was important to Solon that no one "remain impassionate and insensitive to the common good" (Plutarch's words).[37] I doubt Madison would support an edict like Solon's that could so exacerbate factional passions, and, certainly, mandatory political action would today hardly be prudent. But there is a sense in which Solon's mandate trumps Madison's fear of factional strife. Political apathy and indifference are, for the most part, more deleterious to the public good of a democratic republic than public confrontation over conflicting interests. No less than Rosa Parks's civil disobedience, Solon's "middle way" could serve as an example for civic interaction. Just as the civil rights heroine's act of disobedience opened the way for mass participation in the Montgomery bus boycott, so Solon's heroic effort at formulating the Athenian legal code was followed by his renowned self-imposed exile, so that the citizens might learn to rely not on a single individual but on the laws and on themselves. We cannot imitate the great Athenian lawgiver, any more than we could repeat the historically more contemporary act of our American heroine. But Solon's way could inspire, I think, some Solonic reflections on the state of the American polity. In what follows I will offer some brief, inchoate, and incipient thoughts in that vein.

Charting a true middle course in today's uncertain political waters involves, among other things, a vigilant tacking between the swirling vortex of relativism and the harsh rocks of ideology. Both of these extremes have the effect of obviating any need for practical wisdom. In a relativistic framework there can be no "right" act, save, perhaps, the rightness of diversity; in ideologies there is indeed a right way, but it is known independent of any reality. The time and place are irrelevant, equally so the way an act is done. Ideological purity alone counts. Since I have already dealt extensively with the deficiencies of relativism, in this final section I want to expound a bit on the excessive claims of ideological politics, particularly its expression in a dogmatic moralizing that seems to haunt our politics from time to time.

I noted earlier in this chapter the profound and salutary origin of the civil rights movement in moral principle. Though it had more political overtones than people sometimes acknowledge, it was a movement rinsed through with notions of freedom and justice. The temptation today, for those who assume that legacy, is to see every political issue in simplistic moral terms: good guys vs. bad guys, right vs. wrong, the partisans of liberty vs. the defenders of life, and on and on. This excessive moralizing permeates our public discussions on everything from pornography to foreign policy and makes it exceedingly difficult to negotiate our differences in any creative way. Once the opposition is defined in morally reprehensible terms, no compromise can be effected. Political commentator E. J. Dionne notes that the problem lies with "the best people in politics: the philosophically committed activists left, right and center."[38] What they do, he asserts, is not just argue with opponents but demonize them. "Your adversary can't simply be wrong; he or she has to be a baby killer or a woman hater or a racist or a 'quota queen.' "[39] In this hothouse of moral condemnations, there is little or no room for the creative imagination of practically wise actors such as Rosa Parks or Solon. Dionne concludes: "We have to ask whether the nastiness of public life is undermining our very capacity for self-government—whether the toll we're exacting falls . . . on our ability to reason together, which is what republican government is supposed to be about."[40]

Given the highly intricate and complex nature of political issues today, it is easy to appreciate the temptation of moral reductionism. Citizens who tried to decipher the debate about nuclear defense and proliferation of weapons easily got lost in the miasma of technical language and strategy options. More recently, the environmental debate exposes citizens to the same conundrum. Is there really a "greenhouse" effect on the earth? How quickly is the ozone layer being depleted? Who's responsible for pollution of our waters— watermen blame farmers, environmentalists blame watermen, farmers blame environmentalists. The cacophony of debate leaves the ordinary citizen bewildered. It is easier to retreat into a comfortable moral enclosure where a course of action is predetermined. If nature is my god, I spike the trees; if progress is my dogma, I thwart the "kooks" of the environmental movement at every turn. For the partisan of the middle way, however, there are few if any shortcuts to sound judgment. Good public policy depends on an enlightened citizenry.

It is not my intention to diminish the importance of moral commitment here. I simply want to point out that the texture of political policy is much more open-ended than moral ideologies of both left and right would allow. A liberal colleague of mine once seriously argued that no moral judgment can *ever* be made about those caught up in the web of inner-city drugs and violence. They are all victims, he said. I doubt that such a judgment could be made on the basis of any real experience with drug dealers, and my colleague's unabashed amoralism is most vigorously rejected by inner-city mothers of slain innocent victims. On the other hand, it seems remarkable to me that conservatives and neo-conservatives alike— who quite understandably, I think, point out the evils of sexual license—seem to have a huge blind spot to the enormously pervasive vice of greed. Inside-trading scandals, corporate takeovers, advertising pandering, loss of Sabbath and Sunday to buying and selling—all these excesses are rationalized away as mere "blips" or artifacts on the healthy cardiogram of a robust capitalism. I suppose none of us are free of ideological blinders; they, too, Madison would surely aver, are part of our nature. Solon's example of operating out of a moral principle like justice, all the while keeping open to the possibilities in a situation, seems to offer some hope of a remedy. The ideologue acts with one goal in mind, the establishment of his or her moral order. The classical statesman like Solon acted out of a principle (*archē*) that served as a beginning and guide for action. A politician committed to the public good will want to address the issue of the federal deficit. I doubt there is an a priori solution available to such a person. Resolving the problem of the national debt involves a great deal of practical imagination and an understanding of the policies that Americans can best accept. In this matter, a Solonic solution may well be elusive; but an ideological one will surely be disastrous. If ideological walls are to be breached, a willingness to see things as they are and an eagerness to engage all citizens in conversation are absolutely essential.

The problem today is, in part, that a whole generation of Americans learned politics in the crucible of the protest movements and in opposition to them. To be political today is either to express oneself in self-righteous outrage or engage in the nasty realpolitik of gaining political control and keeping it. The middle way becomes an ever narrowing path.

Plutarch says of Solon that he adapted the laws to reality rather than reality to the laws.[41] That, actually, is a good starting point. For example, we are not ever going to extinguish pornography, and efforts to do so are more likely to end up extinguishing some important civil liberties. But neither do we need to be complacent about the spread of obscenity. And surely some regulation of it is not an unrealistic goal. Abortion is another, more intractable example. It too is likely to remain with us, but it hardly seems defensible to protect it as an untrammeled constitutional right.

I do not imagine that any suggestions I might have for a middle way will go unquestioned. But my purpose has not been to analyze specific issues but to mine the underlying assumptions of a good polity that will allow constructive debate to continue. What this book calls for is a renewed willingness of citizens to be political, to engage other citizens on a broader patch of road called the middle way, to argue out our differences, and to act accordingly. We need to return to what E. J. Dionne has aptly called that "old-fashioned sense of common civic endeavor."[42] It is time to put aside the self-righteous politics of moral superiority and willingly work with each other in a true spirit of compromise. Unless we can com-promise, promise with each other, there will be no common purpose left to unite us in the face of overwhelming diversity. What we promise with each other is a fidelity to the principles that constitute the American polity: freedom, equality, justice, and, above all, the public good.

Neither Beasts nor Gods

In a song from one of his recent albums, Bob Dylan recites a litany of modern woes with the accompanying refrain: "We live in a political world." Dylan's view that "politics" is the appropriate name for our dehumanized society is hardly eccentric. Many citizens would prefer an hour in the dentist chair or a class in metaphysics to attending a congressional hearing. Politics is viewed, at best, as an unwelcome burden and, at worst, as an occasion for corruption. We search for meaning and discover fulfillment in our relationships with family, friends, even co-workers; not with politicians. How discordant, then, is Aristotle's refrain: "Human beings are by nature political." To our ears that assertion seems either patently false—can we not be human without being political—or unduly pessimistic—can we not escape the corruption of our nature that is politics?

In this book I have tried to swim, rather doggedly I suppose, against the current of our time by returning to a richer sense of the political that can be found in the classical tradition and by following its sometimes hidden streams that course even today through our public lives. Admittedly, politics has lost that all-encompassing meaning it had for the Greeks. But it is no less true that every flight from the political is defined by the political; freedom from the political is itself a political choice, and every attempt to circumscribe the political can only be executed within a political world. The sense of politics I have argued for encompasses whatever humans do whenever and wherever they come together to determine the substance and direction of their common life. Just as friends go to the movies, business colleagues "do lunch," couples make love, believers worship, so citizens assemble. And wherever they assemble, whether in a legislative hall or in a union hall, in a courtroom or in a boardroom, they share their common concerns and purposes. In short, they form a community. Politics is the activity of public community. Without civic interaction, there would be no schools and libraries, no hospitals and police stations, no museums and theaters, no playgrounds and ballparks. Very little of what we would consider today as essential for a flourishing existence could be accomplished without politics. Aristotle was right: it is good to be political—even if we are not always good at it.

So, there's the rub. Politics is not natural in the way blood courses through our veins or the way our stomachs growl when we are hungry. Rather, it is rooted in the specific human abilities to think and to choose, and so it must be practiced if we are to get good at it. Furthermore, because it is one of the foremost possibilities of our human nature, precisely because it can be such a noble enterprise, the political order is subject to the basest corruption. *Corruptio optimi pessima.* This book could have offered a more extensive account of that darker dimension of politics. That they did not is partly because of my own limitations (I am surely no Sophocles) but also partly (and this may well be a conceit) because I thought that only within a renewed sense of the nobility of the political order could the real tragedy and not just the melodrama of politics be appreciated. Still, it would be well to keep in mind one of the memorable lines from one of the more memorable political characters in American literature, Governor Willie Stark: ". . . from the stink of the didie to the stench of the shroud. There is always something."[1] Robert Penn Warren's masterpiece serves as a bracing reality check for us Americans, obsessed as we can be with our innocence and engulfed as we too often are in our self-righteous posturing that masks our shame over lost innocence.

And yet, even yet, as Willie whispers on his deathbed, "it could have been different."[2] Neither purely innocent nor hopelessly corrupt, neither a choir of angels nor a pack of wolves, neither gods nor beasts: humans are given that in-between space to dwell on the earth and under the sky, with their fellow mortals. To live as best we can on that middle path is, I believe, the timeless task of Western humanity from its origins in Greece to its modern and postmodern expressions. Odysseus stands as the paradigmatic figure in that tradition. After lingering long on Calypso's luxuriant isle, he rejects the goddess's promise of immortality "to see his friends, to return to his high-roofed home and to dwell in his native land."[3] That great conscience of modernity Albert Camus saw Odysseus's choice to return to Ithaca as the authentic human stance: the rejection of "divinity in order to share in the struggles and destiny of all men."[4] Camus's *Rebel* is a marvelous testament to the continuity of the tradition but also, alas, to its dissolution; for, unlike the modern rebel, Odysseus was not rejecting divinity insofar as it implied a divine order and a human piety. The choice to leave Calypso's island inaugurates a new, distinctively human possibility: a *bios politikos*. What he rejects is the totally private and apolitical world of Calypso's cave. Her name means "the hider goddess" and her invitation to Odysseus was not for him to join the council of the gods on Mt. Olympus; rather she offered him the endless pleasures of her bed and board within the dark confines of her cave. Given Odysseus's renowned appetite, this was no meager temptation, and his preparations to leave the island and his crossing to Phaiacia clearly indicate an heroic restraint and a reappearance, even rebirth, into the public life of mortals. What he left behind, then, was an unremarkable private life that lacked the flavor of great deeds and great words. He chose, in short, the mortal life of a community over the life of a satisfied appetite, a beastly immortality.

Today, we luxuriate on our couches in front of the television and with a godlike detachment view the spectacle of human struggle. Channel surfing, interactive videos, and the promise of virtual reality (all surely the envy of the gods) forestall any threat of boredom. Should something bestir us to leave our private caves it most likely would be what Homer called "this cursed belly." We want "a piece of the pie." Today's Odyssey, then, requires us to choose to leave our couches, to curb our appetites and to walk outside where we can encounter a public world where, at its best, citizens interact for the sake of the common good.

We need not travel far: our neighborhood, our local school, church or synagogue, our civic association or city council—wherever citizens gather to speak and act. Throughout this book I have focused on these smaller, more local communities—a Tilghman Island, a Le Chambon, a Montgomery, Alabama—because that is where we can still find Tocqueville's "schools of democracy," that is where we can still achieve a measure of what Thomas Jefferson called "public happiness." When we find such a public community we should hold it, as Edmund Burke instructs us to, in "utter reverence," for there are few gifts or blessings greater than a human fellowship "we somehow haven't to deserve."[5] Perhaps that splendid local actor during the days of the Montgomery bus boycott, E. D. Nixon, said it best:

> I'm an old man now, but I'm so proud that I had a part in what happened here in Montgomery. . . . I figure it was the best thing that ever happened in Montgomery, and I'm proud that I was part of it, even though . . . so many people got famous out of it and I was still left here. And I'm still here servin' the people and the rest of 'em gone. . . . So I'm gettin' more joy out of it now. . . .[6]

Say "Amen," somebody.

NOTES

A Note on the Classical Texts

In the course of writing this book I have consulted numerous texts and translations of the classical authors. Because my purpose has been to open the classical authors to the modern reader and to get us to rethink the basis of our public lives, I have avoided the more technical discussions of textual scholarship. Except where noted, I have used my own translations of the classical authors, not out of any claim to originality but because I found a particular way of expressing the Greek text in English that was conducive to the point being made in the discussion. In addition, I felt at times that a more literal translation of a particular Greek word or phrase would be more helpful in understanding the meaning of the passage.

There are various ways of citing these texts that make for a frustrating inconsistency, partly because the texts themselves are often arranged quite differently by different editors. Citing the chapter of a work is particularly misleading, so I have adopted the standard practice of using the Arabic number to denote the Book, followed by the line numbering developed by classics scholars; so, for example, Aristotle *Politics* 2.1260b36. The more helpful English editions contain this numbering system.

For the Greek and Latin texts the most accessible and user-friendly source would probably be the *Loeb Classical Library* (Cambridge, Mass.: Harvard University Press), which contains the Greek and Latin text with the English translation on the opposite page. These numerous volumes published over the course of this century contain all the major works used in my book. My references are consistent with the *Loeb* editions. One caution, however, is in order: the *Loeb* translations are a help to reading the classical text and hence are not elegant or particularly literary. For English editions of the classical works, see individual notes on specific texts.

INTRODUCTION
Weavers and Sailors

1. Plato *Laws* 9.875b, in *The Collected Dialogues of Plato*, edited by Edith Hamilton and Huntington Cairns (Princeton, N.J.: Princeton University Press, 1973). Weaving as a metaphor for politics can be found throughout the ancient texts. Particularly insightful, or so I found, is Lysistrata's extended metaphor in Aristophanes' great play of the same name.

2. Among any number of various works, I will cite but a few: Robert Bellah, "Creating a New Framework for New Realities: Social Science as Public Philosophy," *Change* (March/April 1985), pp. 35–39; Wendell Berry, *Home Economics: Fourteen Essays* (San Francisco: North Point Press, 1987); Michael Novak, *Free Persons and the*

Common Good (Lantham, Md.: Madison Books, 1989); William Galston, *Justice and the Human Good* (Chicago: University of Chicago Press, 1980); Marcus Raskin, *The Common Good: Its Politics, Policies and Philosophy* (New York: Routledge and Kegan Paul, 1986); and Amitai Etzioni, *The Spirit of Community: Rights, Responsibilities and the Communitarian Agenda* (New York: Crown, 1993).

3. See Walter Lippmann, *The Public Philosophy* (New York: Mentor Books, 1955) and John Courtney Murray, S.J., *We Hold These Truths* (New York: Sheed and Ward, 1960).

4. Richard J. Bishirjian, ed., *A Public Philosophy Reader* (New Rochelle, N.Y.: Arlington House, 1978), p. 18.

5. To cite an example, Marcus Raskin's *The Common Good: Its Politics, Policies and Philosophy* (despite its best intentions) seemed, to this author, to be a case of putting the old wine of leftist ideology into the new wineskin of "common good" language with rather predictable results.

6. For an excellent analysis and thoughtful critique of the whole issue of foundationalism and postmodernism, I would recommend Jerome Miller's *In The Throe of Wonder* (Albany: State University of New York Press, 1992).

7. Murray, *We Hold These Truths*, p. 320.

8. William Sullivan, *Reconstructing Public Philosophy* (Berkeley: University of California Press, 1982).

9. This approach is quite developed in theological circles, inspired chiefly by the works of Stanley Hauerwas, especially *A Community of Character* (Notre Dame, Ind.: University of Notre Dame Press, 1981). In philosophy, Alasdair MacIntyre has done the ground-breaking work in his *After Virtue* (Notre Dame, Ind.: University of Notre Dame Press, 1981). In his later works, however, he considerably revises the more particularist elements of that earlier work.

10. "There exists no 'story of stories' from which the many stories of our existence can be analyzed and evaluated." Hauerwas, *A Community of Character*, p. 96.

11. Robert Sokolowski, *Moral Action: A Phenomenological Study* (Bloomington: Indiana University Press, 1985). Because my purpose as a public philosopher is different from Sokolowski's, I do not strive for the same rigor of analysis that his work so impressively achieves.

12. With respect to the natural law tradition I hope that my own efforts make explicit what is surely implicit in that view: that "human nature" is no abstract extrapolation but rather a concept derived from paying close attention, as Aristotle did, to what it means to be human.

13. My comments here are based on some rather intensive efforts on my own part as member and chair of our own county's "Values Committee" for a number of years.

14. E. J. Dionne, Jr., *Why Americans Hate Politics* (New York: Touchstone, 1991), p. 332.

CHAPTER 1
The Contemporary Scene: A Modern Antigone

1. For the earlier decision by Judge Hews, see *Bouvia v. Co. of Riverside*, No. 159780, Sup. Ct., Riverside Co., Cal., Dec. 16, 1983; for the later decision by Judge Deering, see *Bouvia v. Superior Court*, 179 No. B019134, Cal. App. 3d 1127, Apr. 16, 1986. Redirected, June 5, 1986. Other details of this case have been gleaned from numerous news reports. For analyses of the case, George Annas's reports in the *Hastings Center Report* have been most helpful. See "When Suicide Prevention Becomes Brutality: The Case of Elizabeth Bouvia" (April 1984), p. 20ff.; "Elizabeth Bouvia: Whose Space Is This Anyway?" (April 1986), pp. 24–25; and "Transferring the Ethical Hot Potato" (February 1987), pp. 20–21. For my own analysis, which differs somewhat from Annas's, see "What Nurses Profess: The Elizabeth Bouvia Case" in *Health Progress* (July/August 1985), p. 52A, and "Keeping Elizabeth Bouvia Alive for the Public Good" in *Hastings Center Report* (December 1985), pp. 5–8. See also Sr. Corrine Bayley, C.S.J., "The Case of Elizabeth Bouvia: A Strain on Our Ethical Reasoning," *Health Progress* (July–August 1986), p. 40ff.

2. *Newsweek*, January 16, 1984, p. 72.

3. For the classic use of the phrase consult *The Federalist Papers*, No. 10.

4. Beginning with the *Griswold v. Connecticut* (1965) decision which struck down laws forbidding distribution of contraception, a relatively uncontroversial decision, the right to privacy has been subsequently invoked in a number of crucial cases, most notably the abortion decision *Roe v. Wade* (1973) and the Quinlan case (1976). For treatment, see Germain Gabriel Grisez and Joseph M. Boyle, *Life and Death with Liberty and Justice*, (Notre Dame, Ind.: University of Notre Dame Press, 1979), pp. 50–55, 96–99. For its use in the Bouvia case, where the court speaks of a "fundamental right to protect what little privacy remains to her," consult Annas's article "Transferring the Ethical Hot Potato" (see note 1).

5. Even the earlier ruling of Judge Deering against Bouvia's claim and in favor of High Desert Hospital—predicated as it was upon his agreement with hospital officials that Ms. Bouvia was still intent upon her own suicide (despite, I should mention, considerable evidence to the contrary)—did not so much reject her right to refuse treatment as it affirmed the higher claim of the state to preserve life.

6. Murray, *We Hold These Truths*, p. 85.

7. According to Strauss, we muddle along "sane and sober when engaged in trivial business" until we confront a crucial issue [like Bouvia] and then we "gamble like madmen." When forced to inquire into our ultimate standards we actually find only "our blind preferences." Leo Strauss, *Natural Right and History* (Chicago: University of Chicago Press, 1950), p. 4. There is a subtle but fateful shift from reason as the grounding source for individual rights to reason as the instrumental force in satisfying individual desires. Once reason becomes instrumental to a more fundamental will or desire the very structure on which individual rights was built collapses. See William Sullivan's *Reconstructing Public Philosophy*, pp. 18ff. and 39ff., for an extensive discussion of that fatal flaw.

8. Sophocles, *Antigone* 472. Translation by R. C. Jebb, in *Seven Famous Greek Plays* (New York: Random House, 1950). I cannot here go into an extended interpretation of the *Antigone*, but it seems to be the best scholarly view that Sophocles is presenting a dramatic conflict in which the demands of the state and family shatter against each other because of some very real flaws in the characters of Creon and Antigone. For support of my interpretation of Antigone, see William F. Zak, *The Polis and the Divine Order* (Lewisburg, Pa.: Bucknell University Press, 1995), ch. 2.

9. "Fulfilling one's responsibility for a person's welfare differs in important respects from fulfilling a person's rights. To do what a right-holder demands may be inconsistent with one's responsibility to him; for giving someone what he has a right to may in fact not be good for him at all—indeed it may be quite harmful." John Ladd, "Legalism and Medical Ethics," in *Professional Ideals*, ed. Albert Flores (Belmont, Calif.: Wadsworth Publishing Co., 1988), p. 100.

10. *Washington Post*, February 12, 1984, B5. (Emphasis mine.) Daniel Callahan notes, in another context, how rights language tends to cut short moral analysis: "It is the great missing link in recent discussions of the rights of competent patients: what should be done with the rights once one has them." *Setting Limits: Medical Goals in an Aging Society* (New York: Simon and Schuster, 1987), p. 176.

11. I call her a "modern Antigone" because, unlike her ancient counterpart, she appeals to her own, not her family's interest. Still, like Bouvia, Antigone's familial interest is (for the Greeks at least) private, and, more importantly, Antigone seems more intent on affirming her own will in opposition to Creon's than on being a spokeswoman for the family. How else to explain her insensitive treatment of Ismene?

12. *Bouvia v. Co. of Riverside*.

13. John Stuart Mill, *On Liberty* (New York: W. W. Norton, 1975), p. 11; and David Hume, "On Suicide," in *Ethical Choice*, ed. R. N. Beck and J. D. Orr (New York: Free Press, 1970), p. 73.

14. Jeremy Bentham, *Principles of Morals and Legislation* (Oxford: Clarendon Press, 1907), ch. 3, sec. 1, p. 24.

15. See note 1. Also, Judge Hews made a similar argument in his opinion.

16. *Bouvia v. Co. of Riverside.*

17. Gordon Wood, *The Creation of the American Republic* (Chapel Hill: University of North Carolina Press, 1969), p. 55.

18. In her *On Revolution* (New York: Viking, 1963), Hannah Arendt makes a solid case that the founders had "much to lose in terms of private interest" (p. 133). See also Walter Lippmann: "These struggles are at once too general and too passionate to be explained in the ground of calculated self-interest. Man responds to the cause of liberty who can never hope to enjoy its fruits. So it must be that the tree of liberty has its root in some deep and abiding need of man." *The Essential Lippmann: A Political Philosophy for Liberal Democracy*, ed. Clinton Rossiter and James Lare (New York: Random House, 1963), p. 131.

19. *The Federalist Papers*, No. 45. See also No. 10, where the "public good" is continually invoked as the regulatory idea of any state.

20. Strauss, *Natural Right and History*, p. 5.

21. John Locke, *Second Treatise on Government*, in *Political Writings of John Locke* (New York: Mentor, 1993), bk. 2, ch. 2, no. 6, p. 264. Though Locke justifies slavery that results from a forfeiture of the right to life as occurs in a criminal act or act of war, his principle remains that it is just as wrong to *willingly* enslave oneself as to kill oneself. Contrast this view with Hobbes's in *Leviathan* (Baltimore: Penguin, 1968), ch. 20.

22. Of course, there is a vocal minority of thinkers who continue the tradition, but their success is severely limited by the "apparent" necessity of having to accept an Aristotelian and Scholastic "baggage" in order to enter into the conversation. I say "apparent" because I hope to demonstrate that the notion of natural law is not an extrapolation from a teleological metaphysics but embedded in our very relationships and discourse.

23. I have in mind here not just pluralism as a political theory but also a position one finds increasingly in theological circles: the despairs of any common public square and a retreat instead into the *ecclesia* or "communities of character" (admirably described in the writing of Stanley Hauerwas). Surprisingly, even the writings of Germain Grisez, coming as they do out of the natural law tradition, seem to drift to a libertarian viewpoint, but only out of a practical, not theoretical, exigency. There is much to be learned from these voices, but I will argue against their contention that, either for theoretical or practical reasons, we can no longer speak and act in terms of the common good.

CHAPTER 2
The Public Good: The Greek Mean or Goldilocks's Chair

1. Aristotle, *Politics* 2.1260b36–1261a. For an English edition of the works by Aristotle cited in this chapter, consult *The Basic Works of Aristotle*, ed. Richard McKeon (New York: Random House, 1970). The word Aristotle uses for beginning—*archē* —suggests not just the start of the investigation but also its guiding principle. For the importance of this sense of beginning, see also Aristotle, *On Sophistical Refutations* 183b20–27.

2. See John Rawls, *A Theory of Justice* (Cambridge: Belknap Press of Harvard University Press, 1971), ch. 3.

3. Robert N. Bellah et al., *Habits of the Heart* (Berkeley: University of California Press, 1985), pp. 75–84.

4. Ibid., pp. 82–83.

5. Ibid., p. 84.

6. Here I would recommend C. S. Lewis's watershed work, *The Abolition of Man* (New York: MacMillan, 1947). Despite the volumes written on reproductive technologies since the publication of this work, it remains the most insightful analysis of that horrifying vortex.

7. See Hannah Arendt, *The Human Condition* (New York: Doubleday Anchor, 1959), pp. 10–11.

8. Emily Dickinson, *Complete Poems*, ed. Thomas H. Johnson (Boston: Little, Brown, 1960), no. 113.

9. The examples are Aristotle's. See *Politics* 1.1253a9 and *Nichomachean Ethics* 9.1170b13–14. See. also Plato, *The Laws* 2.666.

10. *The Philosophy of Edmund Burke* (Ann Arbor: University of Michigan Press, 1970), p. 49.

11. Aristotle, *On Sophistical Refutations* 183b25. The translation is Sokolowski's.

12. Aristotle, *Nichomachean Ethics* 9.1170b12.

13. Murray, *We Hold These Truths*, p. 6.

14. The distinction is found, of course, earlier in Plato and throughout the tradition. Contemporary phenomenologists have noted even further refinements of that distinction that need not be discussed in this context. But see Sokolowski, *Moral Action*, ch. 3.

15. In fact, as Hadley Arkes points out, an alliance could even be formed among enemies or, at least, radically divergent states as in the United States' and Russia's SALT treaties. See *First Things* (Princeton, N.J.: Princeton University Press, 1986), pp. 15–19.

16. *Politics* 3.1280b3–5. If a lawgiver focuses only on warfare and the *survival* of the polis, "he will never make a statesman in the true sense" (Plato, *The Laws* 1.628d).

17. See also Cicero, *De Officiis*, 1.44, 158, where he argues that even if by a magic wand all our needs were taken care of, we would not thereby rush into the solitude of contemplation but would seek the company of others.

18. Burke, *The Philosophy of Edmund Burke*, p. 43.

19. I am indebted again in this section to Robert Sokolowski's excellent treatise, *Moral Action*, especially pages 59–60.

20. *Politics* 1.1252b29. The word means literally "its own or self-sustaining principle or beginning," and should not be confused with autonomy—*autonomos*, "a law unto itself."

21. Murray, *We Hold These Truths*, pp. 7–8.

22. Aristotle's phrase encompassed more than just strictly political exchanges. He recognized the power and importance of such social bondings as *phratria* (today's Lions, Elks, Moose, etc.), *thusiai* (religious communities), and *diagōgai* (athletic clubs). *Politics* 3.1280b37.

23. See *Politics* 2.1261a32 and *Nichomachean Ethics* 5.1133a2, where the term is explored in more detail. It bears mentioning that while the term "reciprocal equivalence" seems to bear no particular gender or race bias in and of itself, Aristotle limits it to citizens, who were of course only free and male.

24. Burke, *The Philosophy of Edmund Burke*, p. 44. Jacques Maritain is even more effusive:

> Thus, that which constitutes the common good of political society is not only the collection of public commodities and services—the roads, ports, schools, etc., which the organization of common life presupposes; a sound fiscal condition of the state and its military power; the body of just laws, good customs and wise institutions, which provide the nation with its structure; the heritage of its great historical remembrances, its symbols and its glories, its living traditions and cultural treasures. The common good includes all of these and something much more besides. . . . It includes the sum or sociological integration of all the civic conscience, political virtues and sense of right and liberty, of all the activity, material prosperity and spiritual riches, of unconsciously operative hereditary

wisdom, of moral rectitude, justice, friendship, happiness, virtue and heroism in the individual lives of its members. For these things all are, in a certain measure, *communicable* and so revert to each member, helping him to perfect his life and liberty of person. *The Person and the Common Good* (Notre Dame, Ind.: University of Notre Dame Press, 1966), pp. 52–53.

25. Maritain, *The Person and the Common Good*, p. 53.

26. For an excellent treatment of the various meanings of the word "nature" and its appropriateness for the understanding of politics, see J. Budziszewski, *The Resurrection of Human Nature* (Ithaca: Cornell University Press, 1986).

27. Stephen Tonsor, "What Is the Purpose of Politics," in *A Public Philosophy Reader*, p. 270.

28. In chapter 4 I deal with the particular difficulties of articulating a rhetoric of the public good in a pluralist society.

29. For an exhaustive treatment of this sense of the political I can think of no better work than Hannah Arendt's modern classic, *The Human Condition*. In his seminal work, *The Resurrection of Nature*, Budziszewski offers a further distinction that relates to the level of involvement in the political:

> The weak form [of Aristotle's definition] is that human beings cannot develop fully and properly unless they care in some way for the common good as well as their own affairs, and along with this that they faithfully discharge their responsibilities as citizens. The strong form is that political "activism" is the only admissible form of political practice and the very substance of the good life. (p. 109)

The latter, which he calls "Ciceronian," is the vocation of a few; the former, the responsibility of us all.

30. These many senses of politics create a rather striking analogy, I would suggest, to the "many senses" of being outlined by Aristotle according to the *pros hen equivocal* in the *Metaphysics*.

31. Michael Walzer, *Spheres of Justice* (New York: Basic Books, 1983), p. 281. In this whole section, I am both indebted to and critical of what Walzer calls his "radically particularist view." Even he recognizes the undeniable superiority the political represents in distributing goods, and also assumes, as he says, "the recognition of one another as human beings, members of the same species . . . bodies and minds and feelings and hopes and maybe even souls" (p. xii).

32. Sokolowski, *Moral Action*, p. 177.

33. Ibid., p. 180.

34. Hannah Arendt, "Public Rights and Private Interests," in *Small Comforts for Hard Times: Humanists on Public Policy*, ed. Michael J. Mooney and Florian Stuber (New York: Columbia University Press, 1977), p. 103.

35. Note that the laws as the embodiment of assessments need not contain just negative prohibitions (e.g., not to murder, rape, and steal) but may also include positive injunctions (e.g., to provide food, clothing, and shelter).

36. "Law is nothing else than the rational ordering of things which concern the common good." *Summa Theologica* II–I, q. 90, art. 4. Not every moral assessment of course needs to be captured by the law, as Aquinas noted in q. 96, art. 2.

37. Sokolowski, *Moral Action*, p. 178.

38. Aristotle notes that the law, since it contains no passion, is on that account superior to men (*Politics* 3.1286a18–20). For a wonderful modern account of that ancient wisdom, see Walter VanTilburg Clark's *The Ox-Bow Incident* (New York: New American Library, 1960), ch. 2, which even recreates the encounter between Thrasymachus and Socrates. More relevant here, though, would have been the possibility in that novel that the mob had *not* made a mistake and actually lynched the guilty parties.

39. Plato, *The Laws* 4.713–715. See also 9.875a-b.

40. *Bouvia v. Superior Court of Los Angeles*, p. 23.

41. Though not explicitly stated, the judge's appeal to the "state's interest" (a legal term I am not wholly happy with) certainly catches the notion that private rights can be limited by a public good.

42. "The reckless pursuit of private interests in the public-political sphere is as ruinous for the public good as the arrogant attempts of government to regulate the private lives of their citizens are ruinous for private happiness." Hannah Arendt, "Public Rights and Private Interests," p. 104. See also Jacques Maritain's excellent little essay "Truth and Fellowship," in *On the Use of Philosophy: Three Essays* (Princeton, N.J.: Princeton University Press, 1961), p. 18, where he notes that a society with no substantive beliefs would "condemn itself to death by starvation" because it could not "live without a common practical belief in those truths which are freedom, justice, law and the other tenets of democracy."

43. Daniel Callahan, "Minimalist Ethics," *Hastings Center Report* (October 1981), p. 20.

44. Murray, *We Hold These Truths*, p. 84. I might mention here that, because of the arguments marshaled in this section and throughout the chapter, I cannot agree with

Germain Grisez's and Joseph Boyle's contention that for prudential reasons the argument in favor of the inviolability of human life must be given up in favor of solely appealing to violations of liberty and justice to demonstrate the wrongness of assisted suicide. See *Life and Death with Liberty and Justice* (Notre Dame, Ind.: University of Notre Dame Press, 1979), pp. 46–50. Despite their impressive work, I fear they give away too much and end up with a libertarian position that seems aimed at protecting the security of an embattled sect within a Godless and immoral nation. I don't think we have reached that point and it may well be equally imprudent to concede it now.

45. *Bouvia v. Co. of Riverside.*

46. *Bouvia v. Superior Court* (1986). See also Timothy Cook's article "A 'Dangerous Intrusion' into Private Lives," *The Philadelphia Inquirer* (July 22, 1987), 19-A.

47. Sokolowski, *Moral Action*, p. 178.

48. For the more practical implications as they might have impacted, in devastating fashion, on handicapped persons, see my *Hastings Center Report* article cited in chapter 1, note 1.

49. I am well aware that some in the right-to-life movement and in the euthanasia cause lump all these together for their own purpose. But I think that is a mistake. We can make the distinction between the universal proscription against the direct taking of innocent human life and the conditional obligation to utilize whatever means are available for continuation of life. So, for example, we would not be obliged to utilize an artificial heart even if it were the only means available to sustain life. Cases like Nancy Cruzan are admittedly difficult to read; some see withdrawal of artificial hydration and nutrition as killing while others (like myself) see it as a nonobligatory, inefficacious treatment. The borderline cases do not, however, obviate the distinction made in common medical practice and in the natural law tradition.

50. See Grisez and Boyle, *Life and Death with Liberty and Justice*, ch. 6.

51. Strauss, *Natural Right and History*, p. 134.

52. Grisez and Boyle, *Life and Death with Liberty and Justice*, p. 29. See the entire section B, pp. 25–34.

53. "Human rights do not mean, as some confused individualists have supposed, that there are certain sterile areas where men collectively may not deal at all with men individually. We are in truth members of one another, and a philosophy which seeks to differentiate the community from the persons who belong to it, treating them as if they were distinct sovereignties having only diplomatic relations, is contrary to fact and can lead only to moral bewilderment. The rights of man are not the rights of Robinson Crusoe before his man Friday appeared. They stem from the right not to be dealt with arbitrarily by anyone else, and the inescapable corollary of the rights of man is the duty of man not to deal arbitrarily with others." *The Essential Lippmann*, p. 173.

54. I am most grateful to my colleague Dr. William Zak for this insight into Sopho-clean tragedy.

CHAPTER 3
Public Virtue: The Cyclopes Meet the Eastern Shore Watermen

1. For the Cyclopes story, see the *Odyssey* 9.105ff. Among a number of excellent English editions, I would recommend the latest translation by Fobert Fagles, *Odyssey* (New York: Viking Penguin, 1997), and Robert Fitzgerald's translation, *The Odyssey* (New York: Vintage Classics, 1990).

2. Sophocles, *Antigone* 332ff.

3. The image recalls Nietzsche's characterization of the thinker who dwells alone on the lofty mountain peak. He too is without law, beyond good and evil—a curious and, I think, instructive comparison.

4. By contrast, in popular legend he was said to be enamored of the nymph Galatea.

5. Odysseus himself, it should be noted, was hardly the perfect guest. As soon as he enters Polyphemus's cave, he and his men begin to plunder it. Not that good manners would have altered Polyphemus's behavior; the world of the cave is an eat or be eaten world. But Odysseus is clearly "troubled" by his own appetite, this "cursed belly" as he often remarks, and the *Odyssey* is the story of his instruction in the ways of self-restraint. For an enlightening discussion on the connection between Odysseus's name and his troubles, see George E. Dimock, Jr., "The Name of Odysseus," in *Homer: A Collection of Critical Essays*, ed. George Steiner and Robert Fagles (Englewood Cliff, N.J.: Prentice-Hall, 1962), pp. 106–121.

6. Besides the now classic treatment of the Chesapeake Bay, *Beautiful Swimmers* by William Warner (Boston: Little, Brown, 1976), there are several works that capture the spirit and culture of the Tilghman Island watermen, most notably Mike Blackestone, *Sunup to Sundown: Watermen of the Chesapeake* (Washington, D.C.: Acropolis Books, 1988) and Randall Peffer, *Watermen* (Baltimore: Johns Hopkins University Press, 1979). A splendid pictorial account with engaging quotes from watermen can be found in John Hurt Whitehead, *The Watermen of the Chesapeake Bay* (Richmond, Va.: Tidewater Publishers, 1979).

7. Wendell Berry, *Home Economics: Fourteen Essays*, p. 182.

8. *Odyssey* 9.120–125.

9. For analysis of these informal codes in a similar environment, see Lawrence Taylor, "The River Would Run Red With Blood: Community and Common Property in an Irish Fishing Settlement," in *The Question of the Commons: The Culture and Ecology of Communal Resources*, ed. Bonnie J. McCay and James M. Acheson (Tucson: University of Arizona Press, 1987), pp. 290–310.

10. Hadley Arkes, *The Philosopher in the City* (Princeton, N.J.: Princeton University Press, 1981), pp. 23–24.

11. Ibid.

12. Sophocles, *Antigone* 355–356. I do not think "political virtue" is too much of a distortion of the Greek. Literally the phrase means "those dispositions that protect the city."

13. For Tocqueville's treatment, see *Democracy in America*, vol. 2, bk. 2, chs. 1–9. Page numbers in the text are from the Vintage edition, translated by Reeve and revised by Bowen. Tocqueville is, of course, not the only "modern" to argue that the tradition of public virtue must be substituted by some other, more realistic, consideration. Thinkers from Machiavelli and Hobbes to B. F. Skinner and Edmund Wilson have sought shortcut substitutes for the difficult task of educating in virtue. What makes Tocqueville more interesting, in my opinion, is that he has such an appreciation for the very tradition which he sees as lost. For modern substitutes for virtue, see Yves Simon's helpful little work, *The Definition of Moral Virtue* (New York: Fordham University Press, 1986), ch. 1.

14. At the end of the *Crito*, Socrates shows Crito the disadvantages of criminally violating the laws and still attempting to instruct his children and fellow citizens. In his *De Officiis*, Cicero devotes the final book (III) to the reconciliation of the *bonum utile* with the *bonum honestum*.

15. Quoted in Blackestone, *Sunup to Sundown*, p. 45.

16. Ibid., p. 42.

17. Hannah Arendt, "Public Rights and Private Interests," in *Small Comforts for Hard Times*, p. 105. Arendt allows, in another sense, that the jurors are interested in the case but it is not a private interest and their interest is in "something in regard to which they are disinterested."

18. I am sure Aristotle saw this virtue corresponding to the "reciprocal equivalence" (analyzed in chapter 2) that characterized civic transactions.

19. Philip Hallie, *Lest Innocent Blood Be Shed* (New York: Harper and Row, 1979), p. 286.

20. Mary Midgley, *Can't We Make Moral Judgements?* (New York: St. Martin's Press, 1991), p. 154.

21. For the Kitty Genovese incident, see Martin Gansberg, "38 Who Saw Murder Didn't Call Police," in *Vice and Virtue in Everyday Life: Introductory Readings in Ethics*, ed. Christina Sommers and Fred Sommers (San Diego: Harcourt, 1989), pp. 51–54.

22. Hallie reports conversion was ruled out by Trocmé, who operated by the following principle: "Help must never be given for the sake of propaganda; help must be given only for the benefit of the people being helped." *Lest Innocent Blood Be Shed*, p. 55.

23. Hallie recounts that Trocmé was not even convinced that there was an afterlife (*Lest Innocent Blood Be Shed*, p. 53).

24. Walzer, *Spheres of Justice*, p. 62. The phrase has been used by any number of recent authors.

25. In Latin, *hostis* originally meant "stranger" and later came to mean "enemy."

26. *Odyssey* 13.180–181. Translation is by W. H. D. Rouse, *Homer: The Odyssey* (New York: New American Library, 1937), p. 151.

27. *Odyssey* 14.57–58.

28. Walzer, *Spheres of Justice*, p. 32.

CHAPTER 4
Public Speech: The Barbarian in the Brooks Brothers Suit

1. Christopher Dickey, "Death in El Salvador," *Washington Post*, July 13, 1980, p. A8.

2. Ibid.

3. Aeschylus, *Agamemnon* 430 and *Libation Bearers* 67. There are a number of excellent translations of the *Oresteia* trilogy (*Agamemnon*, *Libation Bearers* or *Choephoroe*, and *Eumenides*); among them I would mention Richard Lattimore's translation in *Aeschylus I: Oresteia* as part of *The Complete Greek Tragedies*, ed. David Grene and Richard Lattimore (Chicago: University of Chicago Press, 1963). I offer a more detailed analysis of the trilogy, particularly the *Eumenides*, in my article "*Peitho* and the *Polis*," *Philosophy and Rhetoric* 19, 2 (1986), pp. 99–124.

4. Alexis de Tocqueville, *Democracy in America* (New York: Vintage Books, 1945), vol. 2, p. 149.

5. Heidegger's translation of *deina* as "strange" carries Sophocles' ambiguity about humanity much better, I think, than the customary translation of "wonderful." See Martin Heidegger, *An Introduction to Metaphysics* (New York: Anchor Books, 1959). p. 123ff.

6. The Greek is νόμους γεραίρων χθονὸς / θεῶν Τ᾿ἔνορχον δίκαν.

7. *Antigone* 354–357.

8. Isocrates, "Nicocles or the Cyprians" 6–7 and repeated in "Antidosis" 254. See also Aristotle's *Politics* 1.1253a.

9. Quoted in Thomas Gilby, *The Political Thought of Thomas Aquinas* (Chicago: University of Chicago Press, 1958), p. 250.

10. Murray, *We Hold These Truths*, p. 7.

11. Ibid.

12. Ibid. p. 12.

13. Aristotle, *Rhetoric* 1.1356a13.

14. In this connection see William Lee Miller, *Of Thee, Nevertheless, I Sing: An Essay on American Political Values* (New York: Harcourt Brace Jovanovich, 1975) pp. 8–11. I am also deeply indebted to Professor Miller for his comments and gentle critique of an earlier draft of this chapter.

15. Ibid., p. 9.

16. Hans Georg Gadamer seems to be making a similar point about the insufficiency of the logical refutation of relativism in *Truth and Method* (New York: Crossroads, 1988), p. 406ff. However, I think he underappreciates the logical refutation which as a propositional argument does refute the propositional assertion of relativism. His hermeneutical stance does not cancel out what he calls the "relationship of propositions" so much as it *undergirds* it. When Gadamer says, "The consciousness of contingency does not do away with contingency," that surely is a *true* proposition.

17. On the inescapability of political judgment, see Ronald Beiner, *Political Judgment* (Chicago: University of Chicago Press, 1983); see especially pp. 6–8.

18. "In the prevailing popular culture all philosophies are the instrument of some man's purpose, all truths are self-centered and self-regarding, and all principles are the rationalization of some special interest." Lippmann, *The Public Philosophy*, p. 89. Lippmann's diagnosis of modern political life still bears reading even today—thirty years later.

19. Fortunately, this position, once the lonely prerogative of classical and natural law theorists, is becoming more accepted by other philosophical traditions, most notably phenomenologists and even structuralists like Jurgen Habermas. Habermas is particularly important because of his efforts to delineate certain universal and transcendental conditions of any linguistic communication, among them the recognition of the claim of truth and shared values. See Jurgen Habermas, "What Is Universal Pragmatics?" ch. 1 in *Communication and the Evolution of Society* (Boston: Beacon Press, 1979).

20. I am indebted, for this line of analysis, to Robert Sokolowski's penetrating work, *Moral Action*, especially ch. 3.

21. Chaim Perelman, "The Philosophy of Pluralism and the New Rhetoric," in *The New Rhetoric and the Humanities* (Boston: Reidel Publishing Co., 1979), p. 63. Unless otherwise noted, all references to Perelman will be from this work and pagination will be included in the text. Perelman credits his former teacher Eugene Dupreel for his insights into and justification of a pluralist society.

22. Chaim Perelman, "Concerning Justice," in *The Idea of Justice and the Problem of Argument* (London: Routledge and Kegan Paul, 1963), p. 56.

23. See especially Michael Walzer's excellent discussion, "The Problem of Citizenship," in *Obligations: Essays on Disobedience, War, and Citizenship* (Cambridge: Harvard University Press, 1970), pp. 203–225.

24. Perelman's reading of *Antigone* is decidedly modernist. In chapter 2 we analyzed the self-annihilation that could occur when a political community, standing for nothing, lies at the mercy of modern Antigones who seek the satisfaction of their desires.

25. Chaim Perelman, "Rhetoric and Politics," *Philosophy and Rhetoric* 17, no. 3 (1984): p. 131.

26. Ibid., p. 132.

27. Ibid.

28. Again, I am indebted to Robert Sokolowski for this example. See *Moral Action*, p. 65.

29. Murray, *We Hold These Truths*, p. 9.

30. Perelman, "Rhetoric and Politics," p. 133.

31. Murray, *We Hold These Truths*, p. 10. Murray's sound common-sense judgment has recently found strong support from both the phenomenological (see Gadamer, *Truth and the Evolution of Society*, especially chs. 1 and 3), and the Kantian tradition (see Habermas, *Communication and the Evolution of Society*, especially chs. 1 and 3). Ronald Beiner's *Political Judgment* offers an instructive synthesis of both traditions, all the while agreeing with the point of Murray's that consensus lies at the heart of disagreement:

> There must be underlying grounds of judgment which human beings, *qua* members of a judging community, share, and which serve to unite in communication even those who disagree (and who may disagree radically). The very act of communication implies some basis of common judgment.

... The very possibility of communication means that disagreement and conflict are grounded in a deeper unity. (p. 143)

32. George Weigel, *Catholicism and the Renewal of American Democracy* (New York: Paulist Press, 1989), pp. 148–149.

33. George Weigel, *Tranquilitas Ordinis* (New York: Oxford University Press, 1987), p. 179.

34. For its role in the public debate and particularly within the religious tradition, again see George Weigel's thoughtful treatment in *Tranquilitas Ordinis*, especially pp. 243–248.

35. On this point I am also indebted to George Weigel's argument in *Catholicism and the Renewal of American Democracy*, chs. 8 and 9. I would stress perhaps more than he does the intellectual dissimulation among conservatives as much as liberals.

36. That is not the case with the tradition. One *locus classicus* is Aquinas's *Summa Theologica* II-II, q. 64, art. 7: "Is it permissible for someone to kill another in self-defense?"

37. I have in mind here an ecumenism described by Richard Neuhaus as "the engagement of disagreements within the context of mutually respectful conversation." See his *The Catholic Moment* (San Francisco: Harper and Row, 1987), p. 94 and also sections 19 and 20.

38. See the first page of chapter 2.

39. *The Challenge of Peace* (Washington: U.S. Catholic Conference, 1983), #74, p. 24. This document is instructive because it has become a touchstone not only within the American Catholic community but in the public forum as a whole. It is clearly the Bishops' position that both the just-war theory and pacifism have a moral legitimacy and share certain common convictions. However, the two positions are left pretty much side by side and little is said about how they ought to interact with one another or how two such mutually opposed understandings of the act of killing might be reconciled.

40. There are some "pacifists" who say they would be willing to kill in self-defense but not in war (a sort of state pacifism) and some just-war theorists who are willing to kill noncombatants though usually under very strict exceptions. Even here lines are still being drawn though I confess I hardly know how such modifications could be justified within the principles implied by both pacifism and just-war theory.

41. Friedrich Wilhelm Nietzsche, *The Gay Science* (New York: Random House, 1974), no. 228.

42. Letter to John Reynolds dated Sunday 3 May 1818, in *John Keats: Selected Poetry and Letters* (New York: Holt, Rinehart and Winston, 1965), p. 317.

43. See Karl Rahner and Herbert Vorgrimler, "Evangelical Counsels," in *Theological Dictionary* (New York: Herder and Herder, 1965), pp. 155–156.

44. See Paul Ricoeur's "Non-violent Man and His Presence to History," in *History and Truth* (Evanston: Northwestern University Press, 1965), pp. 223–233, for how that tension can be creative, although Ricoeur's identification of violence with history is I think overly romantic and neglects the overwhelming evidence of the acceptance of nonviolent practices in civil and political life.

45. Beiner, *Political Judgment*, p. 186.

46. *The Essential Lippman*, p. 480.

47. Aristotle, *Nichomachean Ethics* 9.1167a20–1167b15.

CHAPTER 5
Public Action: Rosa Parks and Two Very Old Dead White European Males

1. Quoted in Harold Raines, ed., *My Soul Is Rested* (New York: G. P. Putnam, 1977), p. 41. For an account of these events, see Taylor Branch, *Parting the Waters: America in the King Years, 1954–1963* (New York: Simon and Schuster, 1988), ch. 5, and Martin Luther King, *Stride Toward Freedom* (New York: Harper and Row, 1958). I will rely heavily on both works throughout this chapter.

2. It is probably impossible to single out any specific event as the beginning of the civil rights movement. Civil rights activities go back much further than 1955, but Rosa Parks's act is as good a place as any to mark the birth of a national movement.

3. Aristotle, *Nichomachean Ethics* 6.1139a5–15. All references in the text are to book 6.

4. "Zeus himself ordained law for mankind. As for fishes and beasts and winged fowls, they may feed on one another without sin, for justice is unknown to them. But to man he gave the law of justice." Hesiod, *Works and Days* 276–279, quoted in *The Presocratics*, ed. Philip Wheelwright (New York: Odyssey Press, 1966), p. 26.

5. Aristotle's general definition of prudence is "a rational disposition for attaining the truth in acts that are good or bad for a human being" (1140b6–7). Later on in book 6 he discusses how that is specifically accomplished by "deliberating well" (*euboulia*). Excellence in deliberation is defined as "a correctness about what is feasible at the right place (*hou*—where), in the right manner (*ōs*—how), and at the right time (*hote*—when)" (1142b27–28).

6. The phrase is Martin Luther King's in *Stride Toward Freedom*, p. 19.

7. Sokolowski, *Moral Action*, p.33.

8. I am indebted here and throughout this chapter to Hannah Arendt's great work *The Human Condition*, especially ch. 5, "Action."

9. Quoted in Branch, *Parting the Waters*, p. 139.

10. Aristotle, *Rhetoric* l.1356a.

11. Sokolowski, *Moral Action*, pp. 70–72 and p. 38.

12. Aristotle, *Nichomachean Ethics* 6.1139a24–25.

13. King, *Stride Toward Freedom*, p. 36.

14. Ibid.

15. Ibid.

16. Ibid.

17. E. J. Dionne, Jr., *Why Americans Hate Politics* (New York: Touchstone Books, 1991), p. 337.

18. Arendt, *The Human Condition*, p. 168.

19. Throughout this next section I am again indebted to Hannah Arendt's ideas, particularly her *On Violence* (New York: Harcourt, Brace and World, 1969).

20. Aristotle, *Nichomachean Ethics*, 1140b9–10.

21. Augustine, *The City of God* 12.20, quoted in *The Human Condition*, p. 157.

22. Hannah Arendt, *Crises of the Republic* (New York: Harvest Books, 1969), p. 69ff.

23. For Le Chambon, see chapter 3.

24. Aldon Morris, *The Origins of the Civil Rights Movement: Black Communities Organizing for Change* (New York: Free Press, 1984), p. 73.

25. Martin Luther King's difficulties in Chicago might be attributable, in part, to the inappropriateness of applying the southern experience of the SCLC to the urban scene.

26. Arendt, "Civil Disobedience," in *Crises of the Republic*. "Dissent," Arendt notes, "implies consent and is the hallmark of free government . . ." (p. 88). Civil disobedience, she argues, is appropriate only when the normal avenues for change are blocked (p. 74).

27. For Solon's writings I have used the collection in the *Loeb Classical Library: Elegy and Iambics*, vol. 1 (Cambridge: Harvard University Press, 1931), pp. 104–155. For accounts of Solon, I am indebted to Plutarch's *Lives* (*Loeb Classical Library*, no. 46, pp. 405–499) and Werner Jaegen's *Paideia: The Ideals of Greek Culture* (New York: Oxford University Press, 1939), vol. 1, ch. 8.

28. Plutarch's *Lives*, p. 438.

29. *The Federalist Papers*, No. 10.

30. J. Budziszewski, *The Nearest Coast of Darkness* (Ithaca: Cornell University Press, 1988), p. 26.

31. Plutarch's *Lives*, p. 448.

32. Ibid., pp. 452–453.

33. Ibid., p. 442.

34. Ibid., p. 417.

35. Aristotle, *Constitution of Athens* 8.5. Cicero makes a similar complaint about the noninvolvement of citizens in *De Officiis* 1.20.68–70.

36. Aristotle, *Constitution of Athens* 8.5.

37. Plutarch's *Lives*, p. 456.

38. E. J. Dionne, Jr., "The Politics of Nastiness," *Washington Post*, July 27, 1993, A17.

39. Ibid.

40. Ibid.

41. Plutarch's *Lives*, p. 464.

42. Dionne, *Why Americans Hate Politics*, p. 337.

CONCLUSION
Neither Beasts nor Gods

1. Robert Penn Warren, *All the King's Men* (San Diego: Harcourt Brace Jovanovich, 1946), p. 191.

2. Ibid., p. 400.

3. *Odyssey* 5.42–43. The words, interestingly enough, are uttered by Zeus.

4. Albert Camus, *The Rebel* (New York: Vintage Press, 1956), p. 306.

5. Burke, *The Philosophy of Edmund Burke*, p. 43. The final phrase is borrowed from Robert Frost's "The Death of the Hired Man."

6. Raines, *My Soul Is Rested*, pp. 37, 50.

INDEX

Rick Maloof

Francis Kane teaches political philosophy, biomedical ethics, and ancient philosophy at Salisbury State University in Maryland. He has published articles in the *Hastings Center Report*, *Philosophy and Rhetoric*, *Commonweal*, and *Religion and the Intellectual Life*. His book reviews have appeared in the *New York Times Book Review*, *America*, and *Vogue*. Active in his community, he coaches soccer and has helped develop a nationally recognized policy for teaching about religion in the county school system. He and his wife are the parents of five sons.